KEPPLER
ON THE
EYE LEVEL
REFLEX

TEXT AND
PHOTOGRAPHS
BY HERBERT KEPPLER

A frank, bold,
irreverent analysis
of today's
most discussed
camera type
and its use, with pungent
advice, and
critical remarks
whenever appropriate

For Louise

PREFACE

Warning to the reader: this is not an objective book. It is opinionated, sassy, and as the cover says, frank and irreverent. It is also fun to read and packed with information. It is filled with marvelously informative charts, diagrams, tables, testing methods and all that technical know-how one would expect from Burt Keppler. It is also filled with some of the best photographs taken by one of the best photographers I know. But this is about the only page in the book that will tell you a little about its author, who—in addition to being opinionated, sassy, frank and irreverent—is also curious, warm-hearted, articulate, humorous and about the most completely informed person around when it comes to single-lens reflexes. Keppler got to be an authority in photography by the one sure path—working at it. To begin at the beginning, he was born with a camera in his eye, hypo in his blood, since his father is the distinguished photographer Victor Keppler. From the age of 6, when Burt got his first camera, till now, some 30 years later, he has been taking pictures. He first toddled into a darkroom when he was 8. When he was in prep school he was the tireless president of the camera club (I know one of its members). And throughout all the years since, whenever he has a nervous tic he takes it out by snapping a shutter. This has kept him from taking up smoking but has not prevented him from sharing his photographic experience by writing on photography. As a matter of ridiculous statistical fact, I have just figured out that in the decade plus that Burt Keppler and I have worked together on *Modern Photography* magazine, I have read, edited and okayed well over a million words of his delightful prose. (I'm not bored yet.) During those years, I have watched him grow from low man on the editorial totem pole to second in command, as Executive Editor. In this time, he has lost a little hair, but gained a wife and child. When I first knew him he drove a rather dilapidated Singer; nowadays it's a bright shiny Mercedes. He has moved from a small flat in Greenwich Village to a rather elegant house in the Westchester suburb of Croton-on-Hudson. Those million words plus I was talking about have spanned an important decade in photography. They have dealt with equipment, materials, techniques, with the lives of important photographers (who can forget the superb piece on Dr. Roman Vishniac?), with books (a truly cutting edge on his reviewer's sword), with fun (the time we had a lens made from a milk bottle). After all this, I still pick up each page of a Keppler manuscript with the same sense of anticipation I give to a Keppler-cooked meal. This is considerable. *Keppler on the Eye-Level Reflex* and Keppler on *boeuf bourguignon* are both fine stews. I'm sorry you can enjoy only one.

JACQUELYN BALISH
Editor, *Modern Photography*

ACKNOWLEDGMENTS

Thanks to my good friend Ernest G. Scarfone, Modern Photography magazines's art director, who designed this book page by page, to Bennett Sherman whose precise, clear drawings and technical aid grace these pages, to Maynard Wolfe, Y. Ernest Satow and Edward Meyers, three photographer friends who kindly allowed the author to use a number of their functional photographs, to Norman Rothschild, single lens reflex enthusiast, whose filter chart is on pages 46 & 47. To Dr. Max Wirgin of the Exakta Camera Co. who first insisted I try a single lens reflex, to Bob Tenney and Bill Daly, Minolta Reflex men always ready with a willing ear for complaints and suggestions, to Ralph Lowenstein, a fine engineer, designer and enthusiast of Miranda Co., to Joe Ehrenreich, Joe Abbott and Len Silverman, the knowledgeable, hard working and imaginative force behind Nikon Inc. And very special gold medals to two singular gentlemen, Everett Gellert and Augustus Wolfman, publisher and Editor-in-Chief, respectively, of Photography Publishing Corp., and Modern Photography Magazine, for their willingness to back this opinionated author whenever he could prove he was right, if not wise. Without them, he would never have had the opportunity to acquire the information in the book, no less print it.

CONTENTS

INTRODUCTION

It's snowing. The brownish winter landscape is receiving a clean coat. New impermanent forms have appeared. Drifts on the windswept terrace table resemble the arch of a gothic cathedral. Azalea twigs stab upward creating angular black lines against the snow. In summer it will long be gone, replaced with buds, insects and my daughter in a sunsuit not yet bought. It seems only yesterday she was born but the time elapsed is 24 months and a few thousand pictures. These have recorded Kathy's gradual recognition of the world and it of Kathy. Gray adds highlights to my wife's hair and this too is a photogenic miracle. Every contour, every line, every expression has at some time passed through one or another of my lenses. We have gone on trips together, stayed home together, entertained friends together, watched birds together. These have all been mirrored faithfully by my camera. I have not done nude studies, photographed the president of the United States, Marilyn Monroe or the World Series. For me my subjects are closer, more personal and far more rewarding and important. The pictures and words in this book which I am now completing record nothing more exciting than my world as imaged through the eye-level reflex camera. I believe that this design can best overcome the technical recording complications that stand between you and your own world. Nothing short remains between what you want to photograph and your ability to carry it out. Herewith we attempt to cover the techniques and supply the information to reach this end.

HERBERT KEPPLER
Croton-on-Hudson, N.Y.

March, 1960

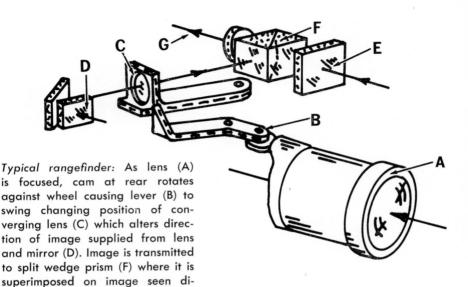

Typical rangefinder: As lens (A) is focused, cam at rear rotates against wheel causing lever (B) to swing changing position of converging lens (C) which alters direction of image supplied from lens and mirror (D). Image is transmitted to split wedge prism (F) where it is superimposed on image seen directly through lens (E) and transmitted through partially silvered mirror in wedge prism (F). When two images coincide, lens is properly focused. This is only one of many similar systems in use.

Logical prism reflex: Image as seen through lens (A) is reflected by mirror (B) upwards and projected onto ground glass (C). Prism (D) redirects image 90° and delivers it to eyepiece (E) where entire area is enlarged for focusing. When shutter release is pressed, mirror (B) will swing upwards causing exact image as seen through prism to be exposed to film. Virtually all reflexes work in this manner. If mirror is properly aligned there is little chance of any mechanical error. You see what you get. You get what you see, no matter what lens is on the camera.

INSIDE

THE

REFLEX

The eye-level single-lens reflex is the simplest, most logical, accurate and exciting type of 35mm camera today. Light from the subject enters the lens, is reflected upwards by a 45-degree mirror through a glass prism and directed to your eye. What you see is an image which in area and perspective is precisely what the film will record. No matter what lens you fit to the camera you can witness the result immediately, since the image projected by the lens itself is your viewfinder. The eye-level reflex has removed all obstacles between you and your subject. Its lens sees as your eye sees; it views the world just as you do.

The rangefinder camera is the only rival to the supremacy of the single-lens reflex. It is smaller because no glass prism or interior mirror is required. The viewing and focusing system, which is separate from the camera lens, is fantastically complex.

As you can see from the illustration the reflex camera viewing system has a direct connection with the taking lens. Instead of showing a constantly bright ever sharp image as do all finder systems other than reflex, you can see just what is sharp and what is not sharp at full aperture. In some cameras there is an automatic stop down button so that you can see the depth of field at the exact aperture that you are using. With finder systems other than the reflex, you can't see what is sharp and what isn't, what is apparently distorted and what isn't. You won't know what your lens actually "saw" until you have the film processed.

Getting back to our own camera, the reflex, let's look briefly at the two basic types.

Focal-plane shutter reflexes: The most versatile and the largest number of single-lens reflexes use a cloth or metal "ribbon" shutter which travels across the back of the camera, just in front of the film plane (diagram bottom page 13). The shutter is made of two or more curtains, with a variable open slit maintained between them, which travel across the film. Different shutter speeds are obtained by altering the size of the slit. The narrower the slit the higher the speed.

Why the focal-plane shutter? Since it is placed towards the rear, it does not interfere with the optics of the camera, and permits the use of an almost unlimited number of different lenses. Detractors claim that the focal-plane shutter is difficult to synchronize with regular or electronic flash. While this has been true in the past, and electronic flash had to be used at low shutter speeds, camera manufacturers have been busy remedying the situation. By increasing the rate of travel of the shutter (not to be confused with shutter speed) the speed at which electronic flash can be used has risen as high as $\frac{1}{125}$ sec. It's also said that the slit type of shutter can cause distortion when shooting action (true, with such shutters in large camera sizes; but almost impossible even to demonstrate in 35mm).

Leaf-shutter reflexes: The most compact and in some ways the easiest-to-use reflexes have a multiple-blade type of leaf shutter located either between the lens elements or directly behind them. While the earliest and least expensive leaf-shutter reflexes did not feature lens interchangeability, some models of the Contaflex do have interchangeable front lens-components and most reflexes with shutters located directly behind the last lens element have completely interchangeable lenses. However, those leaf-shutter cameras offering complete lens interchangeability only offer it in a limited sense. Since the shutter is very close to the back of the lens mount (diagram page 13) lenses must be designed which do not require much rear space—and so far the range of focal lengths available for leaf-shutter reflexes extends only from 28mm to 135mm. Lens makers claim that it is more expensive and far more difficult to manufacture an adequate lens for the leaf-shutter camera than it is to make an excellent lens for the focal-plane shutter cameras. Another disadvantage to leaf-shutter cameras is that they cannot be used for close-up work requiring extension tubes, although portrait lenses can be used with them. (See "Chapter 10" on close-ups for a complete rundown on extension tubes vs. close-up lenses.)

Leaf shutter reflexes have advantages

On the other hand, there are some great advantages to the leaf-shutter cameras. They are easy to hook up with automatic and semi-automatic exposure systems in which built-in exposure meters do all or nearly all the work of setting the exposure controls for you. Also, the leaf shutter can be synchronized at all shutter speeds with both regular and electronic flash.

To sum up, one might say that leaf-shutter reflexes are general-purpose instruments eminently suited to most amateur photographic work. The focal plane shutter camera is more suitable for the advanced photographer who prefers versatility to compactness and convenience of operation.

Whether they come with leaf shutters or focal-plane shutters, all single lens reflex cameras have essentially the same working parts aside from the differences in shutter arrangements (diagrams page 6 and 7).

Lenses: The first eye-level reflex, the 1950 Contax S, used the rather long focal length of 58mm for its normal lens instead of the standard 50mm found on most rangefinder cameras. The 58mm lens proved exceedingly popular, since it provided a life-size image through the finder system and in addition produced an image slightly larger than that made with a 50mm lens. People and nearby objects which often appeared distorted when shot from close-in with a 50mm lens, were improved in appearance when photographed with the 58mm. Actually, it wasn't for aesthetic reasons that the longer focal length was chosen by designers. A 50mm lens would have had to be placed fairly far back in the camera body, and there wouldn't have been sufficient room for the reflex mirror to swing upwards behind the last lens

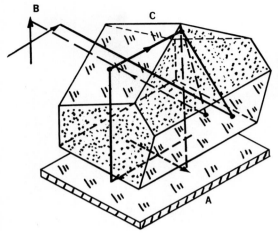

How all prisms work: The image produced on the ground glass (A) is right side up but reversed right to left. The pentaprism (5-sided prism) transmits image right way up (B) but roof edges (C), acting like a mirror, reverse this reversed image.

Three focusing aids: Split prisms (A) provide rangefinder focusing. Plain ground glass ring (B) gives you ground glass focusing. Area outside ground glass (C) has Fresnel rings which brighten glass to the edges but tend to make focusing difficult.

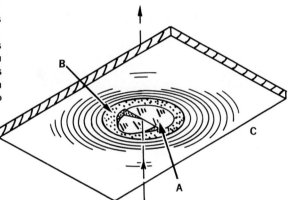

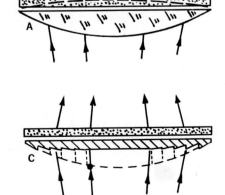

Why the fresnel lens?: Light from lens heads toward ground glass but is converged by field lens (A, top picture). Field lens improves edge brightness of ground-glass image but produces curvature of focus (B) because of central thickness. By substituting plastic Fresnel with ridges (C), each having same slope as equivalent field lens, equal brightness is produced minus curvature of focus.

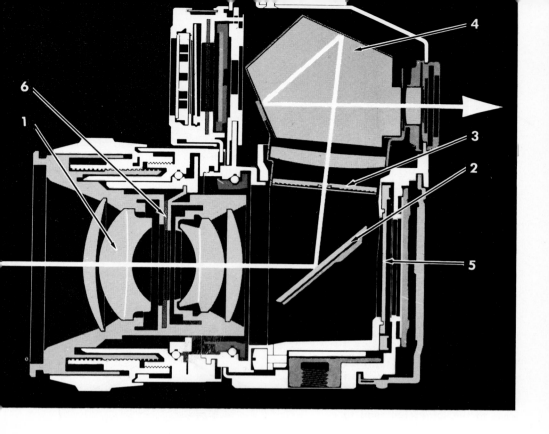

element. By adopting a focal length slightly longer than 50mm, the clearance
was easily gained. Many single-lens reflex manufacturers have continued to
use the longer length with some settling at 55mm and 52mm. If you intend
to do much portraiture and close up shooting, the longer "normal" lens will
probably be best for you. But if you're a scenic and group-picture man, the
50mm lens (yes, they finally solved the mirror-swing problem) may be preferable. The leaf-shutter reflexes are most often fitted with 45- or 50 mm lenses.

The maximum lens aperture is far more important on reflex than on
rangefinder cameras. The brilliance of the viewing and focusing image depend
to a great extent on it. The larger the aperture, the more light reaches the
ground glass screen. Also, the larger apertures produce less depth of field
at any given focusing distance; consequently, the subject image tends to snap
in and out of focus more swiftly. It's easier to find the exact point of sharpness with an f/2 lens than with an f/2.8, and easier with an f/1.4 than an
f/2, on the same camera body. (We add "on the same camera body" because some cameras have inherently better viewing systems than others.)

Lens quality is extremely important, of course. Although I have examined hundreds of lenses for all makes of single-lens reflexes, I have yet to
run across more than a few makes which I would call poor. Remember,
though, that even the best lenses of the same type differ in quality. Run a
check as outlined in "Chapter 4," before growing too fond of any particular
lens. In general, avoid the following normal lenses as being below the quality
of others of the same aperture and focal length: 50mm f/1.9 Meyer Primo-

Focal-plane shutter reflex (left): Light enters lens (1) is reflected upwards by front surfaced mirror (2) through Fresnel brightening lens with split-image rangefinder (3) and then through magnifying condensing lens into pentaprism (4) which inverts image and redirects it through magnifying eyepiece to your eye. Shutter (5) is behind mirror. Lens diaphragm (6) between lens elements. This shows interior of Contarex.

Leaf-shutter reflex (below): Optically the light travels through the lens onto the mirror and to the prism in much the same manner as in the focal-plane shutter reflex but there are mechanical differences. The shutter (A) is between (in some reflexes behind) the lens elements. Since it must remain open for focusing, a separate baffle behind the mirror (B) protects the film until the moment of exposure. This shows interior of Contaflex.

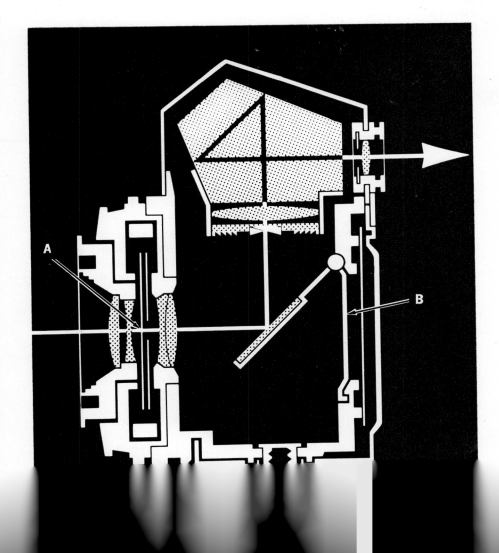

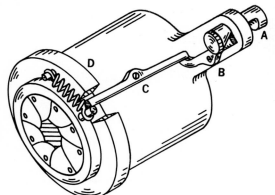

External auto diaphragm: When shutter trip button (A) is pushed inwards against camera body shutter release, an undercut cam actuates lever (B). Lever (C) moved by (B) closes diaphragm. Spring (D) pulls diaphragm back to full opening when shutter trip button is released.

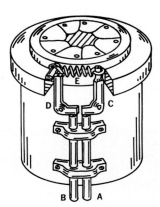

Double-pin auto diaphragm: When camera and shutter are cocked, both pins (A, B) are pressed inwards, holding diaphragm actuating spring (E) under tension. When shutter release is pressed, pin (B) is released allowing spring (E) to close diaphragm. Immediately after exposure pin (A) is released and pin (B) is pressed forward rapidly to reopen diaphragm. Canonflex uses a system which is quite similar to this one.

plan, 50mm f/2.9 Meritar, all 50mm Steinheil Cassars, Rodenstock Trinars, Schneider Radionars, and Meyer Trioplans.

Besides varying in sharpness, lenses also vary in color quality. This becomes obvious if you shoot a lot of color and switch cameras. Suddenly the colors in your transparencies are slightly warmer (more yellowish) or colder (towards the blue) than they were before. While I have never found any modern lenses for reflexes going beyond the limits of acceptable rendition, some color variation between lens makes does occur.

Before leaving lenses, we should mention coating, which is called "blooming" in Great Britain. All modern lenses are coated with a fluoride compound which reduces flare and external and internal reflections. Examine a lens under reflected light and you will note that the surface seems to have a slight bluish cast. Other lenses seem amber. In many lenses the manufacturers cancel out the effects of coating some elements one color by coating other elements another. I have never been able to detect any advantage of amber coating over blue or vice-versa.

Lens Mounts: Most cameras featuring interchangeable lenses use either a screw thread mount or a fast-change bayonet mount. The screw-thread mount is undoubtedly the most secure and the least likely to develop the wobbles after prolonged use; but a screw-thread lens takes longer to change than does the bayonet type, which requires only a split-second short twist of

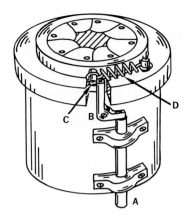

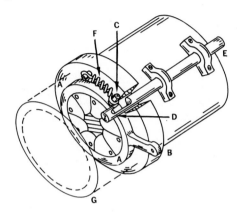

Single-pin auto diaphragm: When release is pressed, internal camera pin presses on actuating pin (A) which, in turn, presses L-shaped lever (B). (B) presses diaphragm ring (C), closing diaphragm. When pressure on (A) is released, diaphragm reopens fully. Praktina IIA works this way. All Japanese reflexes with internal auto diaphragms use similar mechanisms; however, (A) and (B) are replaced by a single lever which moves in a circular direction.

Semi-automatic diaphragm: Diaphragm (A) is opened manually with cocking lever (B). Pin (C) is caught by hook (D). When release pin (E) is pushed inwards by pin inside camera body, spring (F) closes diaphragm. Mechanism is enclosed within lens barrel (G). Edixa, Heiland Pentax, Pentacon, Praktina FX use this system.

the lens to separate it from the camera. Screw-thread mounts on single lens reflexes are pretty well standardized. Many use the Contax S screw thread. Hence many Pentacon, Contax S, and most Edixa, Pentax and Petri lenses can be interchanged with no difficulty.

In the bayonet-mount camp, confusion reigns. The closest to a standard ever achieved is the Exakta inside bayonet mount, which is also used on the Topcon cameras. But other manufacturers felt the mount had too small a maximum diameter and would cause darkening at the finder corners when used with tele and long-focal-length lenses. Therefore the following focal-plane shutter cameras all have their own lens mounts: Alpa, Canon, Contarex, Minolta, Miranda, Praktina, Yashica and the newer models of the Petri and Pentax. Fortunately, many of these do have adapters available so that lenses having Contax S thread mounts or Exakta bayonet mounts can be used on them. It is discouraging, certainly, to learn that if you trade in a camera you may have to unload all your prize lenses as well. Obviously, the situation calls for some careful thought in your original choice of camera. Among leaf-shutter reflexes, there is an even more chaotic fitting problem. No leaf-shutter reflex will accept the lenses of another.

The earliest eye level prism reflex, the Contax S, established a tradition that the normal lenses for these cameras could focus as close as 18 in. Since normal lenses for most rangefinder cameras up to that time—and even today

—don't focus much closer than 3 ft., this feature was greatly appreciated and has been incorporated into practically every single-lens reflex made today. Some lenses go even closer—to 15 in., 7 in., and in the case of the 40mm f/2.8 Macro Kilar, to 2 in.

Some focusing mounts work more smoothly than others. (I don't think anything else comes close to the incredible smoothness of the Zeiss Contarex) but smoothness is not necessarily an indication of excellence or lasting ability. The focusing mount should not be sticky at any point in its distance range. Also, look out for lenses which have a large amount of play allowing you to move the focusing ring back and forth with little or no actual change of focusing. Such lenses can only loosen further. Some can be tightened by a good repairman and others can't.

Most lens mounts are either made of chromed brass or an aluminum alloy, or a combination of both. Chromed brass mounts are usually the best finished, the most rugged and certainly the heaviest. The aluminum alloy lenses are light weight but do not take chroming as well. Consequently they lack the satiny finish of their brassy brothers. Most modern aluminum alloy lenses makers eliminate wear (alluminum is softer than brass) by using brass wherever threaded surfaces are in contact with each other. One method of construction cannot be rated superior to another, but lenses using all brass mount can be quite a load when you are carrying three or four in a gadget bag.

Legibility: a modern camera novelty

Once upon a time all footage, depth of field and aperture scales were engraved in black on a chrome lens barrel. If your eyesight was less than perfect, reading the sometimes almost illegible engravings could be difficult. Then came the Nikkor lenses with their black satin lens mounts and large, easy to read, white or color-coded numerals (picture, page 21). Many other lens manufacturers followed the leader, but some of the white-on-black lens mounts are easier to read than others.

The built-in lens hood on the lens mount of the single-lens reflex is another peculiarity limited to the breed (picture, page 21). The Contax S featured the shade as an integral part of the lens. It certainly made the lens and lens mount impressive in diameter and length. In a more practical sense, it joined the lens and the properly designed lenshood in one unit. Other lens manufacturers adopted the same feature. Recently, starting with the Asahi (now Heiland) Pentax, there's been a swing back in the other direction. The camera and lens, it's contended, are bulky enough. Why make them more bulky? Good shades are available—but as extras. The integral shade does produce its own problems—filters. Because of the shade, a fairly large sized filter had to be attached to the front edge instead of directly in front on the first lens element. And what is needed to shade the filter? Why, another lens shade, of course. Only one lens—the Macro-Kilar—solves the problem by using an inner shade cone which can be removed. The filter is slipped in right close to the front lens element and then the cone is replaced.

Automatic diaphragms: Since the most light reaches the ground-glass screen and pentaprism when the lens is at its full aperture, it follows that the single-lens reflex focuses most easily at full aperture. But before the shutter is released the lens must be closed down to whatever aperture you wish to use for shooting. With the first Contax S, the technique was primitive. You removed the camera from eye level, turned the lens diaphragm to the aperture needed, raised the camera again and attempted to find your subject on the darkened viewing screen.

Shortly after the introduction of the Contax S the first refinement arrived —the preset lens. With it you could focus wide open and then, without taking the camera from your eye, turn a small ring on the lens to close the diaphragm to the aperture which you had previously preset. Turning the ring back opened the lens to full aperture for the next picture.

What's right and wrong with preset lenses

The preset lens had much to do with increasing the popularity of the eye-level single-lens reflex. The famous 58mm f/2 Carl Zeiss Jena Biotar in preset became the standard normal single-lens reflex camera lens. To this day, most long focal length lenses use preset lens mounts.

Obviously, the preset lens was a big step forward but you could still forget to close down the lens, and thus ruin the picture. Opening it afterwards was annoying, particularly to former rangefinder camera owners who were used to doing little but focusing and shooting. Between the time you saw the picture and the time you stopped down the lens and shot, the picture often disappeared.

In the early 1950's the Biotar went semi-automatic, and the completely automatic Contaflex appeared (diagram, page 7). The Biotar for the Exakta, had a small extension which fitted over the front shutter release of that camera. As you press inwards on the shutter release, the spring action causes the lens diaphragm to close to the predetermined aperture. Then a pin at the back of the extension presses the body shutter release, tripping the focal plane shutter. To open the lens to full aperture, you recock the spring using a small lever under the lens. This system is still in use on some Exakta lenses. Similar semi-automatic diaphragms which must be recocked to full aperture are also built into a number of camera bodies (picture, page 14). All of the later-model Contax S and D threaded cameras—Pentacon, Pentax, Petri, and Edixa—have small pins within the camera body which press forward against a diaphragm pin located at the back of the lens mount (picture, page 14). This trips the diaphragm spring and the lens closes. After exposure, most of these lenses has some mechanical means by which you manually reopen the lens to full aperture.

How the automatic lenses work

Photographers who work fast wanted a lens that needed no recocking. Schneider offered the first fully automatic diaphragm for the Exakta. Again an extension covers the camera shutter release button. As you press in the extension, the aperture slowly closes to the opening you have preselected. While pressing in the release, however, you are also compressing a second, slightly weaker spring. When you remove your finger from the release the second compressed spring automatically reopens the diaphragm (picture, page 10). What is the difference? The semi-automatic Biotar closes instantly

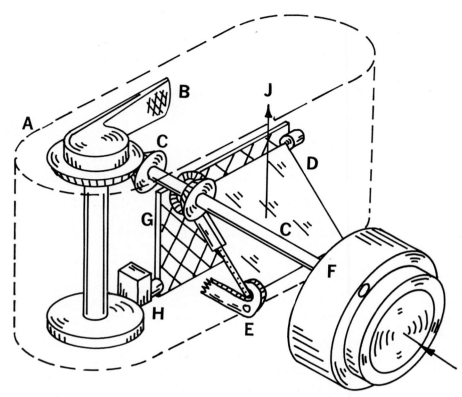

Leaf-shutter reflex: When lever (B) atop camera (A) advances film, shutter actuating shaft (C) brings down mirror (D) which is then held by catch (E). Film baffle (G) covers film, and is held by latch (H). Shutter-cocking shaft enters back of shutter at (F), opens shutter and diaphragm, allowing light to enter lens and be reflected to ground glass (J) and then through pentaprism.

just before the shutter is tripped. It has a gentle easy release, but the diaphragm has to be recocked to full opening afterwards. The automatic Schneider diaphragm closes slowly under slightly greater pressure, but reopens fully afterwards without recocking.

All lenses using an external automatic or semi-automatic diaphragm in the lens mount were invented to adapt older design camera bodies to automatic operation. Most of the more recently designed cameras, however, incorporate automatic diaphragm mechanisms within the camera body. There are three types of internal automatic or semi-automatic diaphragms.

1. Semi-automatic. You must recock the lens to full aperture after each exposure (diagram, page 91).

2. The automatic diaphragm which reopens to full aperture when the film is wound to the next exposure (diagram, page 91).

3. The most automatic lens diaphragm, which reopens fully immediately after the exposure (diagrams, pages 8, 9). This is certainly the most ad-

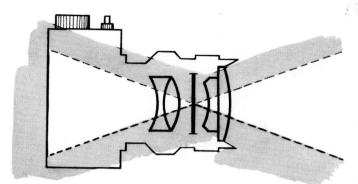

Between-lens leaf shutter: With the leaf shutter between the lens elements, only the front lens cells can be interchanged, thus seriously limiting variety and quality of wide angle and tele lens components.

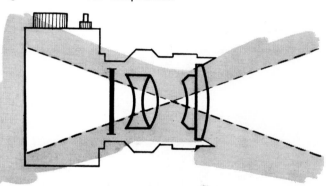

Behind-lens leaf shutter: By moving the leaf shutter behind the rear lens element, entire lens can be removed. Proximity of shutter to rear element limits depth to which an interchangeable lens can be fitted.

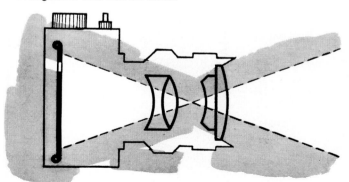

Focal-plane shutter: With shutter at focal plane, interchangeability is vastly improved. Lens designers have easier job of producing variety of good lenses. Only interior mirror (not shown) limits interchangeability.

External auto-diaphragm: Press this plunger and lens will slowly close to predetermined opening. Pin on back of plunger will push body shutter release. When you take finger away, plunger springs out, lens reopens.

An added step: All external and internal semi-automatic diaphragms have a cocking lever such as this which must be pressed sideways after each shot if you wish to reopen lens fully. Lever may also be underneath the lens.

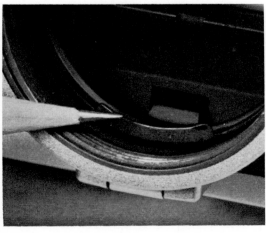

Internal coupling: Internal auto or semi-auto diaphragms must have a pin or lever or collar within the camera body which can activate mechanism at back of interchangeable lens. The mechanics used in various cameras differ.

vanced (and most expensive too). However, more and more reflexes are swinging to it and its's only a matter of time until all have it. The picture through the prism finder remains bright before and after the exposure instead of becoming dark, if the camera has a rapid return mirror.

Unfortunately, there is little standardization in lens mounts and automatic diaphragm mechanisms for single-lens reflex cameras. Briefly, here is the situation. Preset Exakta and Topcon lenses may be used interchangeably. With adapters, these lenses can also be fitted to the Miranda, Yashica, Canonflex, Alpa and Minolta single-lens reflex cameras. Preset lenses for cameras using the Pentacon thread such as the Petri (non-automatic model) Pentax, Edixa, Hexacon can be used interchangeably. Semi-automatic diaphragm lenses using these threads can often be interchanged between the automatic Edixa, Pentax and Pentacon cameras, although some special fittings are sometimes necessary to make the automatic mechanisms connect properly. The preset lenses can also be used on the Miranda and Yashica reflexes with the proper adapters. Automatic Exakta, Topcon Minolta, Yashica, Petri Penta V, Nikon F, Canonflex and lenses for all leaf shutter reflexes can be used automatically only on cameras for which they were designed, with the single exception of the automatic Exakta lenses, which will fit Miranda cameras with the Miranda AXM adapter. If the above seems terribly confusing to you, don't blame me. It's the fault of the various manufacturers, who have not gotten together and adopted a standard size and type mount.

Mirrors: rapid return and otherwise

Mirror: Before the shutter of a single-lens reflex can go into action, the interior mirror must swing out of the way. In early, larger-than-35mm reflexes, pressure on the long-throw shutter release actually supplied the force to raise the mirror. You had to be resolute and swift while pressing the release because your view through the ground glass disintegrated rapidly as the mirror swung upwards. This direct mirror action relied on gravity to bring the mirror down again once you removed your finger from the release. It was simple in construction but the loss of viewing image was disconcerting. Some early 35mm reflexes, the Italian Rectaflex and Swiss Alpa Reflex, nevertheless used such manually-raised mirrors.

The Exakta, even before World War II when it was purely a waist level camera, moved the mirror out of the way in a hurry. When you pressed the shutter release, spring action caused the mirror to fly upwards just before the shutter traveled. The Contax S used such a system. The Exakta still uses it, and most leaf-shutter reflexes use it. Two objections are raised to this action. Some claim that the mirror action causes the camera to jar, making sharp pictures impossible. Careful tests made with single-lens reflexes on tripods and hand-held, however, have failed to provide much evidence to support this theory. All the eye-level reflex camera manufacturers have provided some damping material or mechanism which cushions the mirror as it approaches the up position.

The second objection to the spring loaded mirror is more serious. Once the shutter release is pressed, the finder goes black and the image disappears completely. This prevents photographers from actually seeing the subject at the instant of exposure and after it. It is virtually impossible to use such a reflex for any subject which must be followed in the finder while a series of pictures are made.

The Asahiflex of 1955, caused hardly a stir in the photographic field when it was introduced because it was a waist-level reflex with limited speeds and preset lenses. But it did have one unique feature. When you pressed the shutter release of the Asahiflex, the mirror swung upwards and the shutter travelled, as in the other reflexes. But then the mirror immediately returned to the down position. Because your eye has the ability to retain an image for a short time (the reason why a series of still pictures, when projected in rapid succession is capable of becoming a movie) the Asahiflex user was barely conscious of the fact that the ground glass screen had been black during the actual instant the picture was taken. When the same rapid return mirror was used in the first Asahi Pentax eye-level reflex in 1956, it caused a design revolution. Every professional photographer who had balked at single-lens reflexes because at the mirror black-out bought one even though actually he still could not see the subject at the instant of exposure. There's no doubt in my mind that all future single-lens reflexes will have rapid return mirrors.

Do rapid return mirrors cause jar?

Rapid return mirrors compounded the problems of damping mirror vibration and bounce. The more expensive reflexes have rather comprehensive damping and slowing actions for the mirror. Extensive tests made with the better reflexes fail to show even the slightest unsharpness or camera jar caused by the mirror. In the medium priced cameras, jar and vibration are definitely present, but only before and after the shutter action. If the camera is held firmly in your hands or is mounted on a tripod, the negative image will not lose sharpness because of mirror action.

The mirror position itself is extremely critical, of course. The mirror must move and return to precisely the same spot after each exposure. A slight misalignment, and focus will be affected. Most single-lens reflex focus problems can be traced to the mirror position. In "Chapter 12" you'll find a simple test for alignment.

The Prism: An entire book could be written about pentaprisms—those five-sided pieces of glass which take the reflected image from the mirror, turn it right side up, change it from its reversed position as it appears on the waist-level ground glass, and deliver the image to your eye (diagram, page 5).

The first prism on the Contax S was permanently built into the camera body. The view was life-sized. (If you looked directly at the subject through the viewfinder and kept your other eye open at the same time, the two images were about the same size.) This was caused by a combination of three factors —the focal length of the taking lens, the prism itself and finally the small magnifying eyepiece behind the prism. The central portion of the Contax S viewfinder was acceptably bright but brilliance fell off noticeably in the corners.

The various systems used on today's reflexes to overcome brightness full-off are almost endless. Some cameras have one or more condensing lenses underneath the ground glass. Others use a flat Fresnel field lens which spreads out the light and increases brightness at the corners of the ground glass area (diagram, page 5). When a Fresnel lens is used to brighten the image, the center is generally left clear or a split-image rangefinder included.

A glance through a number of single-lens reflexes will immediately indicate that viewing images vary greatly in size and brightness. Each represents a compromise. Some prisms produce an extremely large-size picture which seems quite close to the eyepiece—often so large and close that eyeglass wearers have difficulty seeing the edges of the viewing image. Other reflexes have a brighter but smaller screen. This is accomplished by using a less powerful magnifier and concentrating more light on a smaller area. Such a screen is more acceptable for an eyeglass wearer since the edges and corners can be seen easily.

Some ground-glass images are produced on very fine screens which seem to improve brilliance. But the exact point of sharpness is often more difficult to find on a fine ground glass than on a coarse screen which actually shows less detail and produces less illumination.

Some leaf-shutter cameras such as the Contarex, Contaflex and Voigtlander Bessamatic have an exceedingly brilliant but non-focusing viewing area. This is achieved by using a brilliant finder which is constantly sharp and cannot be used for focusing at all. These cameras have a central split-image rangefinder surrounded by a narrow ground glass ring, either of which can be used for focusing.

Prism quality itself is a factor in ease of focusing. While the better single-lens reflexes maintain a uniform high standard, the early Contax S cameras varied wildly in prism brilliance and sharpness. Even today, inexpensive, substandard prisms are available for cameras featuring an interchangeable viewfinder system. These prisms are of little value.

Range finder: help or hindrance?

The arguments over the usefulness of the central split-image rangefinder continue. The first single-lens reflex, the Contax S, had a plain ground glass. When the image was sharp, you were in focus. Some photographers claimed (and still do) that they just couldn't be as sure of the exact point of sharp focus as they could with a rangefinder camera. By building two small glass prism wedges into the central portion of the ground glass, an additional focusing system, the split-image rangefinder came into being (diagram, page 5). The split-image rangefinder divides the image on the central portion of the ground glass horizontally in most cameras. When the subject is in focus the two halves of the image match each other. When focus is incorrect, the two image halves do not line up.

Previous rangefinder camera addicts are most enthusiastic over the prism rangefinder. Some reflex men feel that the central rangefinder spoils the clean uncluttered composing area, and in addition, robs them of the best area on which to use ground glass focusing. Certain points are conceded by both sides. The tremendous depth of field of 35mm or wider lenses makes it almost impossible for the reflex user to be certain he has reached the point of sharpest focus. The central rangefinder helps the photographer find this point quickly and accurately. On the other hand, for tele and long focal length lenses the split-image rangefinders are impossible to use. One half or the other turns blank when a long lens is fitted. (The optical reasons for this are interesting but really beside the point). With long lenses the point of sharpest focus can be found without a rangefinder since depth of field is extremely shallow and the picture moves in and out of focus quickly. But for the normal and semi-long lenses, the discussion is pertinent. Personally, I find the rangefinder ground glass almost impossible to use unless I'm focusing on a subject with a straight edge or line which can easily be identified. Just imagine trying to focus on a shaggy dog with a split-image rangefinder and you'll see the problem I feel the rangefinder presents—and can't lick. For wide angle lenses, I concede that a split-image rangefinder may be an aid.

If you're uncertain, choose a camera in which the rangefinder can be added or removed if and when you want. The search for a better central focusing area continues however. The Petri is available with a split-image rangefinder having three areas instead of two. The new Pentax cameras have an unusual central diffraction grid which helps break up the image instantly when it is out of focus. Only an actual trial with a specific system can tell you whether it's good for you.

Is a fixed prism or a removable prism preferable? Despite the various angle finders devised for non-interchangeable prism cameras, the removable prism is more versatile. If you ever intend to mount your camera on a vertical copy stand or do specialized work where interchangeable groundglass inserts would be helpful, the interchangeable prism camera is superior. It is, however, often more expensive and more susceptible to dirt. Even the tiniest speck can become annoying in the viewing system of a single-lens reflex. And there certainly are enough surfaces for dirt to land on—the mirror, the condensing lens, top and bottom, the bottom of the prisms. Taking them all apart for cleaning is a time consuming job. If your photography is limited to general snapshots, the fixed prisms can offer a neat, clean simplification.

Is prism wobble important?

In examining an interchangeable prism camera, you may become slightly suspicious if you notice that the prism doesn't seem to sit solidly but has some wobble. A small amount of movement needn't concern you. It will not affect focus. The critical alignment is lens-to-mirror-to-ground glass. Except in the Exakta, the ground glass screen is not part of the interchangeable prism housing. The prism generally sits on top of it. The ground glass is anchored securely in the camera body.

Shutters: The focal plane shutter of the single-lens reflexes is rather similar to that found on rangefinder cameras. Most of today's better ones are made of rubber-coated cloth or metal "ribbon" or plates, or cloth-covered metal "ribbon." The rubber or metal prevents pinholing. It isn't moths that produce the pinholes. Once upon a time, photographers blamed the direct sun hitting the shutter for the pinholes. But with the mirror of the single-lens reflex in the down position, the sun can't hit the shutter. However, one day I watched a friend smoking a cigarette while changing the film in a single-lens reflex. Hot ashes fell on the cloth shutter. A few days later he was at a complete loss to understand the light streaks in his picture.

An oration could be delivered on shutter speed dial designs. However, it's enough to say that the best dials are single large dials which are easy to read, have equally spaced shutter speeds, and can be set simply by turning in either direction.

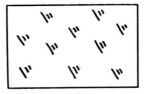

Plain full-focusing finely ground GG

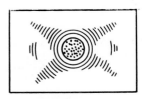

Central fine GG with Fresnel lens

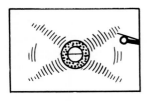

RF with GG collar, mtr. pointers

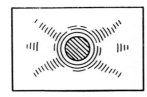

Focusing grid plus full GG area

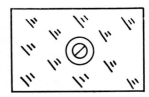

Diagonal RF with full GG

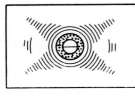

RF, GG collar, non-focusing area

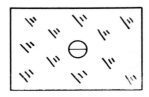

RF plus full GG

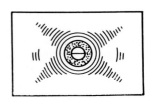

RF, GG collar, clear area, mtr. needle

The leaf shutter, often thought of as far less complicated than a focal plane, is really quite a production (see diagram, page 12) on reflex cameras. A focal-plane shutter simply remains closed, opens during exposure and then closes again. Not so on a leaf-shutter. The shutter must be open to begin with so you can focus through the lens. The diaphragm must be open fully also. Since the shutter is open and can't protect the film, a separate baffle must be used to cover the sensitive material. In some cases, the back of the mirror forms a light trap. You press the shutter release. The shutter must close, the diaphragm close to the right opening, the baffle swing away from the film, and the shutter open and close to make the exposure.

When you wind the film to the next exposure, everything must return to the original position. The baffle recovers the film, the lens reopens fully, the shutter opens. When you realize that the rapid return mirror and completely automatic exposure using a built-in meter will be added to all this, you are left somewhat in awe of photographic automation.

The modern single-lens reflex accomplishing this in a tiny fraction of a second thousands of times in a row shows the camera designer in his finest hour. Oddly enough, the first camera using this principal, the Contaflex, is a model of rugged efficiency.

Camera Body: No element of the single-lens reflex is more important than the camera body. Unless the lens is firmly anchored and parallel to the front, and the film plane machined precisely at the back, all the other features are useless. Many pre-war 35mm cameras were built of stamped steel plates fastened together. While the cameras were small and light, pressure on the camera front or on the back could easily misalign the camera. Fine tolerances were difficult to maintain since each metal part which was fastened to another could add to the error.

Most modern 35mm reflexes are die cast. The front of the camera on which the lens mount is fastened, and the back of the camera where the film travels is really one solid casting. Provided the casting is accurate, a high degree of accuracy can be obtained and maintained. Critical machining and small tolerances generally go hand in hand with camera price. More time can be taken in designing, piloting, manufacturing and inspecting the costlier units. The company can afford to throw more units away which don't quite meet the high standards set for the camera. Someone once said that you don't pay for the camera and lens you get, but for the number of cameras and lenses the manufacturer had to throw out.

Most of today's 35mm reflexes have precise film planes. Once upon a time you knew a 35mm print by the longitudinal scratches the original film acquired going through the camera. Many older cameras had pressure plates which literally crushed the film against the film plane and, naturally, scratched the film. Today's reflexes have a film slot. If you look at the open back you will see four rails running lengthwise. The polished inside rails are slightly lower than the outside (picture, below). The film rides between the two outer rails over the inside rails. The film area on which the picture is formed never touches metal and is therefore never scratched. The film is actually channeled between the pressure plate and the rails.

The take-up spool to which the film is fastened does not actually trans-

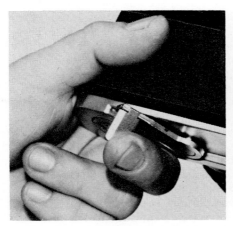

Wind levers: One man's choice is anathema to another. Do you want a top lever, bottom lever or trigger lever? It's a matter of preference.

Camera bodies: Parallel polished rails channel film along solid cast focal-plane in modern reflexes. Sprockets, not spool, drive film.

port the film. It merely takes up the slack from the sprocket wheel drive which also measures off every frame. Some cameras feature takeup spools which wind the film emulsion side out while others wind the film emulsion side in. Extensive use of both systems has failed to prove one better than the other.

Two types of camera backs appear on single-lens reflexes. One swings open on hinges, and remains attached to the side of the camera front. The other back, generally fastened to the bottom plate of the camera, comes off completely. The hinged back is actually more convenient, particularly for loading. There are no extra parts to juggle or keep track of when working in the field; you can change films without even removing the camera from a tripod. Optically and mechanically, however, one type of back does not have an advantage over the other.

Let's look at the pressure plate itself. Some plates are smooth, others fluted or rippled. No single design seems to hold an advantage. Nearly all are of blackened metal, since attempts at using glass or ceramic material resulted in static electric charges being formed when film passed over the plate. As a result, lightning-like static marks appeared on the film. Back to metal went the manufacturers. Why they ever strayed from it remains somewhat of a mystery.

Take-up spools: Removable take-up spools are a pain in the neck. While I appreciate the camera manufacturers' good intentions in providing me with a removable spool so I can replace it with a metal cartridge and have cartridge-to-cartridge feed, thus eliminating rewinding, I think it's a vile idea. The desirability of cartridge-to-cartridge feed is a popular delusion among manufacturers who feel that photographers will go to all the trouble of taking apart an empty cartridge, fastening the leader of film to the spool core and

Lenshoods: Build-in hoods are precise, shield lenses from extraneous light at all times but add to bulk and require extra hood if filter is used.

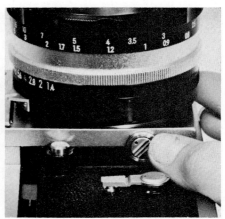

Worthwhile cream: Numeral legibility, button depth-of-field preview mechanism, auto mirror trip (under thumb), cause reflexes to be expensive.

then reassembling the cartridge before loading both cartridges into the camera. Since the film is being fed directly into a cartridge, the manufacturer reasons that the user need not rewind at all. The time and effort spent in scrambling around with the take-up cartridge far exceeds the time and effort needed to rewind the film. In addition, threading a film end onto a spool which slips out of the camera at the most inopportune moments is not my idea of the fun of photography.

Rapid wind levers: A very practical convenience. But wind levers differ radically. Would you find a lever more convenient on top of the camera or on the bottom (see picture page 20)? The best levers are geared, which means that you needn't use one complete throw to advance film and cock the shutter. You can do it in two or more short strokes.

Some wind levers need a shorter single stroke than others. While a short stroke is handy, too short a stroke can put quite a load on the winding gears and require too much thumb pressure for comfort.

The design of the lever itself is worth examining. The lever should pull away easily from the body with just the slightest pressure from the ball of your thumb. Some levers require a fingernail or the tip of a finger to pry them away from the body and are irritating.

Rewind levers: In general, a great convenience. But some are well designed, easy to grasp and turn, others are smallish and slip out of your fingers. Incidentally, don't become a rewind speed demon. Rapid rewinding can cause static electricity marks on the film which may ruin your pictures.

Film counters: Undoubtedly those which automatically reset themselves when you open the camera back are a great help. Breathes there a photographer who has never forgotten to set a manual frame counter and thereby lost track of how much film he's shot?

Shutter releases: These should be smooth and release the shutter fairly close to the beginning of travel. Most people prefer release buttons atop the cameras, but if you use a front body release you may become a great enthusiast for that particular placement.

Preview buttons: A very real advantage if you compose precisely and really care how much of the picture will be sharp at any given aperture.

Are built-in meters any good?

Built-in meters: Professionals may sneer at them but they're still handy. The case against them is clear cut and, in my opinion, slightly ludicrous. Professionals feel that a built-in exposure meter is inaccurate, reduces the camera to an amateur unit and adds additional weight and bulk to the camera. I feel that having a built-in meter is a great aid. Although the separate hand-held meter is certainly more reliable, more versatile and more accurate, the built-in meter furnishes an instant check on your present exposure setting, indicates when the light changes radically, and provides a constant check on the accuracy of your hand-held meter. In addition, how many times have you forgotten to bring your hand held meter? You can't forget the one built into the camera. Most meters seem to fit right into the existing camera bodies. Weight is negligible. One camera to be marketed soon will incorporate a tiny cadmium sulphide cell, powered by a tiny hearing aid battery, reading the central portion of the picture area right through the lens. Thus a photographer will be able to obtain an exposure reading of a distant object through a tele-photo lens. The importance of this type of built-in meter for the serious amateur and professional cannot be overemphasized. Indications are that these highly desirable meters will not necessitate a much larger camera body.

On the other hand, I do regard accessory slip-on or slip-in meters which couple to shutter speed dials, aperture controls or both, real bulky nuisances.

Film type and speed indicators: A great help, I suppose, but not to me until they're made as automatic as frame counters. I always forget to set mine.

Flash sync outlets: Most cameras use the universal European push-on sync connection, one of the most miserable devices ever concocted. Cords become loose and make poor contact, sometimes refusing to connect com-pletely. The individual systems, some with bayonet locks, worked out by several manufacturers for their particular cameras aren't much help either. The connections only fit the flash units made by the camera manufacturers. Camera manufacturers have a talent for turning out flash guns whose versa-tility is often slightly below that of a flashgun for a Kodak Brownie. The manufacturer provides an adapter which allows you to use European push-on connectors and you're right back where you started except you have one more adapter. A better universal system using some type of bayonet lock is surely needed.

Does the camera handle well?

Control convenience: Once upon a time Eastman Kodak Co. placed on the market a 35mm camera to end all 35mm cameras. It was splendidly made, the lenses were excellent, it was far ahead of its time. It had every control known to man and then some—It was an engineer's dream—but not a pho-tographer's. The controls all seemed in the wrong place. They just didn't fall under your fingers where you wanted them. Today's manufacturers attempt to be more logical, but the human element plays tricks on the best of them. What's convenient for a right-eyed, left-handed photographer won't be re-ceived with the same enthusiasm among the left-eyed, right-handed pho-tographers. Camera owners with long thin fingers will rave about a camera which the thick stubby fingered photographer can't control at all. And so it goes—rapid wind lever on top of camera or at the bottom, left hand or right hand shutter release and rapid wind lever, centrally located prism eyepiece or side located eyepiece. There's no one answer. Try out the camera in which you're interested and see.

2

AN
OPINIONATED
CAMERA
GUIDE

I am not equivocating when I insist that it's impossible to name the best single-lens reflex camera. Truthfully, there is no such thing. I can recite the list of single-lens reflexes I have used and liked. A glance at the credit lines under the pictures in this book will reveal that most were taken with Exakta, Miranda and Minolta cameras. Many more would have been taken with the Nikon F if it had been introduced earlier.

My first love was the Exakta because it was the first quality eye-level reflex camera with semi-automatic lenses in a variety of focal lengths. When the Miranda was introduced, I bought it because a lens-mount adapter could be fitted for the automatic and preset Exakta lenses I already owned. Also, I liked the Miranda's quiet shutter; I could use it where an Exakta would get me into trouble. Mirandas made most of the pictures in this book.

When the Asahi Pentax appeared, I both used and admired it but didn't adopt it as my own because it had a Pentacon lens mount which would not accept my Exakta-mounted lenses. On the other hand, the Minolta SR-2 did have an Exakta adapter which enabled me to use my preset Exakta lenses with it.

I had been pestering the Nikon people for years, giving them suggestions for an eye-level reflex incorporating the excellent body and shutter mechanism of their rangefinder cameras. When they produced the Nikon F incorporating most of my suggestions I felt that it was as close as I could come to buying a camera I had designed. Shortly thereafter, the Konica F, Miranda Automex and Topcon C appeared. But you do have to stop changing cameras.

Much depends on you

You'll note that I have left out some important cameras. Here's where the matter of personal choice comes in. I felt that the bottom rapid-wind lever on the Canonflex was very awkward for me. However, I was told recently by a U.N. diplomat that the Canonflex was the only camera he could wind at eye level. He is left-eyed and I am right-eyed.

My friend and colleague at *Modern Photography,* John Wolbarst, insists that he must have a split-image rangefinder and he cares far less about the ground-glass focusing area. I don't like rangefinder focusing, and would rather not have one.

I know that photographers who use electronic flash frequently find leaf shutters essential because focal-plane shutters cannot be synchronized at speeds faster than ⅙₀ sec. or in some few cameras, ¹⁄₁₂₅ sec. They wouldn't touch a focal-plane shutter reflex. On the other hand, I wouldn't touch a leaf-shutter reflex because I do much close-up work using bellows units and a great deal of portraiture using long lenses. You can't fit a bellows unit to a leaf-shutter reflex and the long lenses for the leaf-shutter reflexes seldom focus closer than six feet, which is too far for close portraiture. That eliminates the leaf-shutter cameras for me.

6 steps before buying

Before dealing more specifically with the various camera models, I do want to set down a few principles I think you should follow in purchasing a camera.

1. *Buy from a trusted store*: Pay a few dollars more and get a camera from a local dealer who will treat you as a future as well as a present customer, will service any of your complaints and is sincerely interested in the product he sells. It's far wiser than purchasing a camera at a store where you are unknown and the clerks are interested only in making a quick sale.

2. *Insist on a 10-day money-back guarantee*: The ten days will give you time to test the camera thoroughly and bring it back for exchange or refund if it does not operate properly or you simply discover that you and it are not simpatico. You should also obtain a 90-day guarantee during which time the camera can be returned for at least 70% of its original purchase price. Lastly, insist on a one-year service guarantee to cover all repairs other than breakage or misuse on your part.

3. *Watch prices*: There's nothing wrong with comparing prices at various stores, but settle for store reliability equally with price. Approach sensational camera discounts warily. These often occur just before a new model is introduced and the old discontinued. If you're sure the discounted older model has nearly everything you could possibly want, it may well be a good buy for you.

4. *Check accessories*: If you plan on buying additional lenses in various focal lengths later, make sure that they are available. Treat lenses announced for future introduction as if they didn't exist. Many never will make it. If other accessories, such as motor drives and coupled exposure meters, are important, make certain that these too are available.

5. *Handle as many cameras as possible*: At the photo store, try as many different reflexes as possible. Look through each. Focus and trip the shutter. Is there some other camera you like better than the one you went in to buy?

6. *Take the camera home and test it*: Make tests (see chapter 4).

The following guide to the cameras is in no way intended to replace the beautiful brochures, pamphlets and advertisements which manufacturers, distributors, importers and dealers will gladly shower on your head at any sign of interest. I'm sure that by dropping into your camera store or mailing a short inquiry on a postal card to the various camera concerns you will get all the specifications you need. My main purpose is to pass on my feelings about many of the present cameras' abilities, based on personal experience. Naturally, some cameras I have loved more than others and these affairs will become evident as you read further. Partisans to the contrary, the quality of top Japanese and German mechanical and optical work is about equal.

A heavy, sturdy, somewhat bulky reflex whose convenience in handling will either appeal to you or not. Machining and finish are excellent. This is the only leaf-shutter reflex with interchangeable finders. Model I has waist level finder and non-interchangeable 45mm f/2.8 lens; II is identical to I but has prism instead of waist level finder; III has waist level finder, built-in coupled exposure meter, changeable 50mm f/2.8 lens; IV is identical to III but has prism instead of waist level finder; V is identical to IV but has 55mm f/1.9 lens. Prices vary from about $100 to over $200. Model V is only leaf-shutter reflex with a 55mm lens which makes it a good buy if you want to do much portraiture with a normal lens. The built-in meter seems adequate for most situations except low light. The view through the finder is clear and bright with full focusing ground glass and split-image rangefinder. Normal lenses are very good with 35mm and 90mm f/3.4 accessory lenses superior to many similar lenses for other single lens reflexes. Top shutter speed of ⅟₃₀₀ sec.

Until recently, prism reflex Alpas had a 45 degree viewing angle which required the user to hold the camera below eye level for horizontal shots and stand 45 degrees away from the subject for verticals. To say the least, this was a pesky inconvenience. The current Model 6C, however, has an eye-level prism providing a full, very large ground-glass focusing image and an excellent diagonal split-image rangefinder. The camera is ruggedly built, well finished, has a rapid return mirror, is reliable but bulky. Some controls, such as shutter speed, are downright inconvenient to set if you're in a hurry. The rapid wind lever works in the opposite direction from every other one I know. The 50mm f/1.8 Switar lens in regular mount, or macromount which focuses as close as 7 in. is excellent and other lenses available in special Alpa external automatic diaphragm mounts are also good. The built-in but uncoupled meter is adequate in most situations but not in low light. The camera is relatively noisy in operation. Price of the 6C ranges upwards from $400.

Well-made, average-sized leaf-shutter West German reflex with interchangeable lenses, built-in and coupled meter. The meter needle is visible in the finder. There's a central split-image rangefinder, ground-glass collar, brilliant but non-focusing viewing area. Following the original Contaflex system, the Bessamatic is focused at the center by means of the split-image rangefinder and/or ground-glass collar. Convenience of controls is average. Exposure meter is very easy to use since you needn't take camera from your eye. Sensitivity is quite good even in low light conditions. Normal lenses, either 50mm f/2 or f/2.8, are well above average in quality. The 35mm f/3.5 and 135mm f/4 lenses are also above average. All lenses have an easy-to-use automatic depth of field indicator. There's no rapid return mirror. Bessamatic is only leaf-shutter prism reflex which can be fitted with a zoom lens. The 36- to 82mm f/2.8 Zoomar, although large and slightly unsharp, is quite convenient to use. Prices with regular lenses vary upwards from $200.

Extremely well-built, nicely finished, very automatic focal-plane shutter Japanese reflex. Controls are convenient with exception of 1. folding rapid-wind lever on camera bottom, judged easy to use by some and difficult by others, and 2. depth of field preview control which takes more time to operate than it's worth. Split-image rangefinder and full ground-glass focusing are good size and quite brilliant. Internally automatic diaphragm reopens immediately after shutter action, works with rapid return mirror. Special bayonet Canonflex mount holds lenses securely and can be changed quickly. Exakta lens adapter available. Canonflex 50mm f/1.8 lens vignettes slightly at full apertures. 100mm f/2 accessory lens is splendid and focuses quite close for portraits. Sensitive dual-range meter attaches to front of camera and couples to shutter speed dial, but gets in way of camera operation. Camera looks bulky but isn't. Price at about $300. There are three different Canonflex models which differ in price but little else. One model has a permanent, non-removable prism.

First and original leaf-shutter single-lens reflex, the West German Contaflex is fairly small, well made, nicely finished with controls most conveniently placed. The exposure meter needle of the Super model can be seen through the viewfinder, not in the picture area but to the right of it. Rapid model is same as Super with 50mm f/2.8 Tessar lens, but has no meter. Both feature interchangeable front lens components which are not as small, as convenient or as sharp as completely interchangeable lenses. Something tells me this situation will be rectified soon. If it is and an f/2 model is made available, there may be little reason for considering any other leaf-shutter reflex—unless you don't like the viewing system. It's a central rangefinder and ground glass collar with a brilliant non-focusing total viewing area. Accessories are astonishingly complete, including a monocular attachment which screws directly into lens front to produce the equivalent of a 400mm f/14 lens. Price of Super is about $200, Rapid is slightly less. Cheaper Prima model has poor lenses.

No camera is more precisely machined or finely finished. The view through the non-interchangeable prism is almost blinding in brilliance but, since it uses the Contaflex viewfinder system, a ground-glass collar surrounding a split-image rangefinder, the bulk of the viewing area cannot be used for focusing. The diaphragm is completely automatic, reopening to full aperture when the film is wound. There's a rapid return mirror, and the exposure meter is coupled to the shutter and aperture controls. The needle is visible in the finder to the right of the picture area. It's sensitive, but somewhat difficult to use at first. The excellent 50mm f/2 or 58mm f/1.4 lenses automatically compensate for the exposure increase needed at close distances. This over $400 camera features fine controls but is comparatively large and bulky. Interchangeable lenses in bayonet mount range upwards from 21mm but are somewhat limited in maximum aperture. A simpler, special model without meter but with full ground glass and interchangeable finder is $100 less.

A vast number of lenses are available for this West German-made focal-plane shutter reflex. Camera is available with waist-level finder, with eye-level finder, with and without internal automatic and semi-automatic lens diaphragm coupling. New model Edixa-Mat C and D will have rapid return mirror and fully automatic, instant reopening diaphragm. All models use Pentacon thread permitting very wide accessory lens choice (although a special Edixa with Exakta bayonet mount is available on order). Best standard is 50mm f/1.9 Schneider Xenar. Split-image rangefinder and full-focusing ground glass are adequately bright, camera construction is rugged, but finish is poor. Engravings on models other than Edixa-Mat are hard to see. Shutter speed dials are slightly inconvenient to set, exposure counter must be set manually. Camera is slightly large but fits well into hand. Model D has slow speeds to 9 seconds, is only camera other than Exakta to extend beyond a second. Model C has poor built-in exposure meter.

Body essentially same as 1936 model which shows you how far ahead the East German focal-plane shutter reflex actually was. This is grand old lady of reflexes with fantastic number of lenses available including lenses with external automatic diaphragm from 24mm to 135mm. Best normal lenses are 55mm f/1.9 Steinheil, 50mm f/2 Pancolor and 50mm f/1.9 Schneider. Left-handed rapid wind and shutter release. Fast speeds of VX IIa model are fairly easy to set, slow speeds are inconvenient but extend to 12 seconds. View through prism is moderately bright, split image rangefinder available. Accessories galore. Lower priced simplified camera called Exa II accepts all Exakta lenses. Exakta still does have some features not found on any other cameras such as built-in knife for cutting film, provision for cartridge-to-cartridge feed, stereo system available. This camera is probably most popular single-lens reflex with focal-plane shutter extant. Prices range upwards from about $250. Complete system of accessories is available.

29

This Japanese camera is truly unusual with many unique features. It has an all-metal, six-bladed focal-plane shutter with a top speed of $\frac{1}{2000}$ sec. allowing electronic flash to be shot at $\frac{1}{125}$ sec. (Other cameras limit electronic flash to about $\frac{1}{60}$ sec.) It features a pressure plate which automatically draws back while film is being advanced. (It's claimed that this eliminates any possibility of film scratches but I've never run into this trouble with any modern single lens reflex. If the film is scratched it's usually a faulty film cartridge lip that does it). The Konica has a coupled exposure meter of good sensitivity, an automatic, instant reopening diaphragm, instant return mirror, a split image rangefinder and brilliant ground glass focusing area, a convenient depth of field previewer and a very good 52mm f/1.4 lens in quick change bayonet mount. All this makes the Konica a rather heavy and bulky camera. Not surprisingly this compendium of features sells for slightly less than $400. Smaller, sleeker, meterless Konica S with all meter focal plane shutter is similar to that on F. Price will be less.

At present there are 3 good reliable Minoltas. All have rugged bodies, cloth focal plane shutters with slow speeds from 1 sec., fully automatic diaphragms which reopen when film is wound, rapid return mirrors, hinged back, well marked controls. Prism finder aided by Fresnel lens is bright, focusing easy. SR-1 has 58mm f/2 Auto-Rokkor which isn't quite as good as fine f/1.8 on SR-2 or SR-3. SR-1, 3 have equally spaced speeds on dial which needn't be lifted to be set. SR-2 is oldest model but is good buy because of 58mm f/1.8. If you can persuade dealer to sell this lens with SR-1, you have an even better deal. SR-3 has provision for an awkward accessory meter to couple to shutter speed dial and top speed of $\frac{1}{1000}$ sec instead of $\frac{1}{500}$ as on SR-2. Who needs $\frac{1}{1000}$ sec. Special bayonet Rokkor lenses from 28mm upwards are very good. SR-1 is just over $150.

Only complete focal-plane shutter reflex system featuring two completely different camera designs. Both feature completely interchangeable finder systems. Not yet tested by me, Automex has internal automatic diaphragm with instant return mirror, instant return diaphragm, fairly convenient depth of field preview mechanism. Sensitive, coupled exposure meter with needles visible in viewfinder is handy feature. View through full ground-glass prism (available with and without rangefinder) is fairly bright. Shutter mechanism is exceptionally quiet. Lenses from 28mm upwards are good. Adapters permit use of Exakta, Pentacon preset and manual lenses and special adapter allows automatic Exakta lenses to be used. Miranda itself has special inner screw and outer bayonet mount. Simpler, lighter, quieter D model has no meter but does have instant return mirror, external automatic diaphragm, same quality lenses, same lens adapters, shutter speeds are located on two dials. Automex is around $300. Miranda D is just over $150. Full accessory system is available.

Beautifully made, convenient to use, reliable, reasonably quiet plus an extended array of lenses mark the Japanese-made focal-plane shutter Nikon F as an outstanding camera. The Nikon has an instant return automatic diaphragm, rapid return mirror, convenient depth of field preview button, cloth-covered titanium ribbon shutter and interchangeable ground-glass inserts. You can use the split-image rangefinder or plain ground glass. View is quite bright and reasonably large but concentric rings of Fresnel lens do make focusing except in large central ground-glass area somewhat difficult. 58mm f/1.4 lens is better than the 50mm f/1.4 on rangefinder camera and sharper than 50mm f/2 also furnished. Accessories available include bulk film back, electric motor drive, 85- to 250mm f/4 zoom lens, remote control operation. Accessory meter couples to shutter speed dial and aperture controls, is out of operational way but is somewhat bulky. With f/1.4 lens, Nikon F is under $400.

The original East German focal-plane-shutter reflex introduced in 1949 hasn't changed much. It's still flimsily made, noisy, somewhat unreliable (be sure you test it thoroughly before purchase), with inconvenient controls, and no rapid wind or rewind levers. It has more names than you can imagine—Hexacon, Pentacon Consul, Corbina, Contax D. To confuse matters further, many small model changes have been made to brighten the originally rather dull ground-glass finder and to accommodate an internal semi-automatic diaphragm. Some models have a meter built on top. None have a rapid return mirror. Lens thread is standard Pentacon which allows a vast number of lenses to be used. 58mm Biotar lenses furnished as standard along with 50mm f/2.8 Tessars are sometimes not up to Biotar lenses furnished on other cameras. Despite all, these cameras are dirt cheap selling around $100 and make good extra bodies if you already have a Pentacon threaded camera or are a beginner and don't want to spend more for your first eye-level reflex.

Pentax enjoys fame originally based on the introduction of the first rapid return mirror. The Pentax is a no-nonsense no-frills camera. Its newest models, however, do have fully automatic diaphragms which open immediately after exposure. Other automatic features are kept to a minimum. Controls are very handy, the non-interchangeable prism finder produces a large, bright, ground-glass viewing area with a special light dispersing grid in the center. This grid does make focusing easier. (Whether you prefer it to a camera with split-image rangefinder is a matter of personal choice.) The lens mount on the present cameras uses the Pentacon thread, so besides the large selection of Takumar lenses, a vast number of additional lenses are available. (Newer Pentaxes not yet introduced may have bayonet-type lens mounts of a novel design.) The 55mm f/2 lens furnished as standard is good but not quite the equal of the f/1.8 also available. Machining and finish are about average. Accessory lenses are good but 35mm f/2.3 is unsharp at large openings. Under $200.

Although the designer seems to have missed the boat aesthetically in this Japanese focal-plane shutter reflex, the new Petri Penta V has many features found only on the most expensive reflexes. There's an automatic frame counter, diaphragm with instant return mirror and automatic instant return diaphragm. The shutter is rubberized and the 50mm f/2 lens furnished is quite good. Unfortunately, in an effort to produce a completely automatic diaphragm, the manufacturers have adopted an entirely different lens mount from the earlier model Petri Penta cameras which had preset lenses. Lenses from one model will not fit the other. Controls are convenient on the new V model but lens changing with a permanent revolving threaded collar on the body of the camera is relatively slow. The view through the prism is less bright than in other reflexes. The workmanship is more of the durable than the finely finished variety. Price is slightly more than $150.

This grand old East German focal-plane shutter unit is poorly finished, noisy to wind, lacks rapid wind and rewind levers, doesn't have a rapid return mirror, but it does sport a semi-automatic diaphragm, which must be recocked manually after each exposure, and some fine lenses such as the 55mm f/1.9 Steinheil. It's quite reliable mechanically and has rapid-change breech lock lens mount. Unfortunately, there aren't too many semi-automatic or even preset lenses of different focal lengths available. The view through the finder is adequately bright, the rangefinder and ground-glass focusing area can be interchanged with a plain ground glass. Controls are convenient if not too legibly marked. Accessories including remote control units, bulk film backs and spring wound motors are numerous. In the newer IIA model a completely automatic diaphragm lens system will be available but automatic lenses from one camera model won't work on the other and vice-versa. Preset lenses will work on both. Price of the new IIA has not yet been announced.

A very well made, sturdy Japanese leaf-shutter reflex with built-in and coupled meter, completely interchangeable lenses plus an odd viewing system. Looking through the finder you'll see a large, excellent, central split-image rangefinder. The rest of the ground glass is brilliant but not usable for focusing. You can see the needles for the exceptionally sensitive meter through the prism finder. The outer image area seems to go in and out of focus but the manufacturer warns that it can't be used for accurate focusing. A check with the split-image rangefinder does reveal a discrepancy in focus between the ground-glass viewing area and the rangefinder. The Prismat is not particularly heavy but it's one of the bigger single lens reflexes. Its 48mm f/1.9 lens proves to be exceptionally good and can be focused as close as 18 in. which is unusual in a leaf-shutter reflex although standard procedure in focal-plane shutter reflexes. There's no rapid return mirror. 38mm, 100mm and 135mm accessory lenses were not available when I was examining the camera. Price is over $150.

Built-in and coupled exposure meter, completely interchangeable lenses, a sturdy body and fine finishing characterize this West German leaf-shutter reflex. Some users won't like the bottom rapid wind lever which is characteristic of all Retina cameras. The view through the prism is quite bright especially with the 50mm f/1.9 Schneider lens. The focusing screen is brilliant and the central split-image rangefinder quite helpful. The exposure meter is sensitive enough for even fairly low light conditions but the needle is built into the top of the camera housing. Thus, you can't set the camera at eye level. Lenses interchange rapidly. The 50mm f/1.9 is adequate and f/2.8 is fine but the 28-, 35- and 135mm lenses I've seen were not particularly impressive. Care must be taken to distinguish the S model from the earlier Retina which looks similar but had interchangeable front lens components rather than full lens interchangeability. The meter of the earlier cameras was built-in but not coupled to the camera. Slightly more than $200 with f/1.9 lens.

Well finished, ruggedly built, Japanese focal-plane shutter reflex with excellent 58mm f/1.8 lens. The controls are just where you want them, on both the older model B with semi-automatic diaphragm which must be recocked manually and on new model C with completely automatic diaphragm. These camera bodies seem identical, have rapid return mirrors, easy to throw rapid wind levers, slightly small but brilliant prism finders which are interchangeable, and a good central split image rangefinder. Lenses are interchangeable with all preset Exakta lenses. All semi-automatic model B lenses can be used on C but not vice-versa. New model has instantly opening diaphragm, convenient depth-of-field preview button. Only feature lacking is automatic frame counter. Shutter speed dials are inconvenient to set. Focusing mount of new model C is ribbed in rubber and may be easiest focusing reflex of all. Accessory lenses from 35mm upwards are optically superior. Camera is large. C is over $300. New model is rumored.

The Yashica Pentamatic is a neat, small, well-made, nicely finished focal-plane shutter reflex with controls conveniently placed. The internally coupled automatic diaphragm reopens fully when the film is wound, the frame counter is automatic, there's a rapid return mirror. The view through the non-interchangeable prism is bright. There's no rangefinder. The 55mm f/1.8 lens is outstanding but the 35mm and 135mm preset lenses tested were only acceptable. However, excellent adapters for Pentacon and Exakta lenses are available so you can fit this machine with just about any lens you please if it's manual, preset and in one of these two mounts. The rapid wind lever seems a bit stiff but I could find no trace of film binding causing it within the camera. The shutter is quiet. The frame counter must be set manually. It's one of the few cameras in this price bracket offering a top speed of $\frac{1}{1000}$ sec. Price of the camera is slightly over $150.

3

FILM,
EXPOSURE
AND
NONSENSE

The basic technical aim of every eye-level reflex owner should be to produce pictures of the best possible quality under all circumstances. Shifting from one film to another won't do it. Trading in exposure meters won't do it. Trying the endless array of developers and believing all that's claimed for them won't do it. Only one course of action will: Establish a simple, straightforward film-exposure-developing combination and then stick with it.

As a matter of fact, if you ape the film-exposure-developer techniques of the average magazine photographer you'll soon be sorry. I have found them, with few exceptions to be the most ill-informed, sloppy technicians going. Their best pictures are often saved only by their acknowledged ability to capture subject material that other people can't. As for quality—! Too many professionals follow another professional, the advertising claims of a product or their own mystical intuition.

Before we wade into films, let's examine the basic criteria of quality: fineness of grain and sharpness. We all wish to produce fine-grained, sharp pictures. Unfortunately, fine grain and sharpness do not always go hand in hand. The two enlargements on pages 42 and 43 prove this. One of the large film manufacturers, after much experimenting, came to the conclusion that the contrast between large areas, producing apparent sharpness, was more important to the average viewer than the greater detail produced by fine grain. In addition, a subject photographed by cross lighting which brought out its surface texture tended to appear sharper than the same subject photographed with even illumination on a much finer-grained film.

Use these films normally

Now to specifics. I have deliberately not given an all-inclusive listing of films available. After working with films of many nationalities I've found that trying to deal with too many of the different emulsions available can be more confusing than helpful. We can pare the list down to two or three universally available black-and-white films and with them produce quality photographs of any subject in any lighting condition, from candlelight to brilliant sunshine, with technical excellence equal to that of the best professional photographers. Moreover, by using the same materials constantly, we'll come to know their advantages and limitations, just as we get to know the quirks of an automobile if we drive it a few years.

These startling facts on fine grain and sharpness that I have just mentioned caused me to relinquish the use of an old favorite, Kodak Panatomic-X. For years I exposed it carefully, developed it carefully and amazed my friends with the virtually grainless enlargements that could be made from it. (Many of the pictures in this book were produced this way.) I have now switched to Kodak Plus-X Pan, a semi-fine-grain film with an Exposure Index of 160, which has excellent punch, better edge sharpness, more speed. With Kodak Plus-X Pan there is no reason why you can't safely enlarge your negatives to 11 x 14 or even 16 x 20 with sharp, brilliant results. That's as far as *I* want to go. (If you're in the mood for murals, that's something else. By the way—and this is important: If, in enlarging, you have to crop your negatives so much that you're making the equivalent of larger than 16 x 20 enlargements from a tiny area, there's something wrong with your shooting technique. Move in closer to your subject!)

I am sure that there are many films approaching Kodak Plus-X Pan in quality. But in overall adaptability, ease of handling and availability you will find none. Kodak Plus-X Pan film is remarkably consistent in manufacture, not susceptible to curl, easy to process and easy to have processed by commercial finishers almost anywhere in the world. It's an altogether splendid film, and if you stick with it you'll get to know just what it can and can't do —and it can do most things.

Although I do most of my shooting on Kodak Plus-X Pan, I sometimes need a film with higher speed for low light situations. Kodak Tri-X Pan with an Exposure Index of 400 is just about twice as fast as Plus-X Pan (a difference of one stop—from f/4 to f/2.8, for instance). But the film tends to give an image of slightly lower overall contrast than Plus-X Pan and is therefore easier to print.

Films to use in bad light

For the nearly impossible situation (the wedding in a dark church whose minister won't allow flash, or the hospital nursery which exhibits the newborn babies behind glass in a darkened room) you have your choice of Ansco Super Hypan (E.I. 500), Agfa Isopan Record (E.I. 650), or Kodak Royal-X Pan (E.I. 1600). (Although this last film is not yet available in cartridges in the U.S., it can be bought in bulk and loaded by the user. No doubt it will appear in cartridges soon.) These are amazingly fast films. But even with proper processing, don't expect grainless results. You won't get them. We'll get back to these films in "Chapter 11" when we discuss low light shooting.

How should Kodak Plus-X Pan and Tri-X Pan be exposed? Set your meter at an exposure index of 160 for Plus-X Pan and 400 for Tri-X Pan. Take a reflected light reading *from the darkest area in which you wish to hold detail.*

What about "pushing" film to get higher indexes for shooting in low light? Don't do it. It's more a myth than fact. Photographers who claim fantastic results with super-developers after shooting at indexes of 6000 or so are talking through their nontechnical hats. You can't develop what isn't recorded on the film. What you do accomplish by pushing is to increase negative contrast, overall negative density and graininess. By following my exposure recommendation you'll have well-exposed negatives with plenty of

Why big meters are more accurate: Here's one of the best accessory meters, a Weston Master IV and an extremely good miniature coupled meter which clips onto the Canonflex. Note two intermediate points between all major settings (f/4 and f5./6, for instance) on Weston and none on small meter.

highlight and shadow detail. Give less exposure and you'll start to lose shadow detail. By always reading your meter for the darkest area in which you want to hold detail, you will, in effect be raising the film speed sensibly when dark areas aren't present or important.

I discussed this business of "pushing" films with *Life* Photographer Alfred Eisenstaedt one day. Eisie has shot hundreds of thousands of 35mm pictures in his 30 years of professional photojournalism. An Eisenstaedt picture is distinctive. It is sharp and as grainless as he can make it. Yet he never loses a picture. "How far do you push film speeds when you have to?" I asked. "I don't," he replied. "I rate film close to what the manufacturer recommends." "What happens when you don't have enough light?" I persisted. "I use a slower shutter speed or a wider lens opening," he said. "Suppose you're open all the way?" "I use a slower shutter speed," he insisted. "If you're using the slowest shutter speed possible," I countered. "There is no slowest shutter speed possible," he stated with finality.

Eisie has long practiced and still practices holding the camera steady for exposures of ⅟₁₅, ⅛, ¼ and even ½ sec. For this reason he seldom underexposes film.

To expose film properly you must have a good exposure meter. How

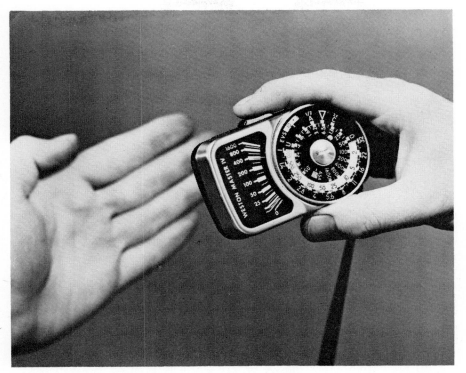

For best color exposure: Flesh tones must be accurate in color no matter what happens in rest of picture. If you can't get sufficiently close to subject to make reading from face, take reflected light reading from the palm of your hand held in same light as subject.

should you choose one? Get the best you can—the Weston Master and General Electric Golden Crown are two meters which are accurate, quite sensitive in low light conditions and have a wide range. This last point is extremely important and not fully appreciated even by people who own good meters. Budget-priced exposure meters and built-in meters often yield readings right on the button: a calculation comes out, say, to f/2 at $\frac{1}{30}$ sec.; a slight increase in light, and the calculation shifts to f/2 at $\frac{1}{60}$ sec. Less light, and the meter falls back to f/2 at $\frac{1}{15}$ sec. The Weston and G.E. meters, however, have more intermediate points. Your chances of maintaining proper exposure are greater with them. Be on the lookout for the new super-sensitive cadmium sulphide meters just introduced. The Gossen Lunasix and Sekonic Microlite are very fine.

Learn to develop your own black-and-white film. While many professional photographers don't maintain a full darkroom, and so send their black-and-white film out for both processing and enlarging to high-priced professional custom labs, few if any commercial laboratories are prepared to develop your black-and-white films with consistency and quality. Even if you can't do your own enlarging, buy a tank and the necessary chemicals for home developing. You can always have a print made over, but if your negatives are ruined there is no redoing them. Anyone can find time and room in kitchen, bathroom or closet for this simple process.

How should the film be developed? If you go along with my Plus-X and Tri-X recommendations, the technique is very simple. Use Kodak Microdol-X developer at full strength. For Plus-X Pan, develop for 14 minutes at 68°F if your subject was photographed in fairly flat lighting. For pictures taken on bright sunny days cut your time to 9 minutes. With Tri-X, develop for 11 minutes at 68°F for flatly lit subjects, and 8 minutes for brightly lit subjects.

Don't try inspection developing unless . . .

I do not recommend that you try developing by inspection. Many professionals claim that they can only get good negatives by taking the film out of the tank during development and examining it under a very dim green safelight, but this system is not for most of us. The professional technicians who can work successfully in this manner spend about one hour becoming accustomed to the dim safelight before they begin processing. They develop many rolls of film, one after another. Their skill, based on experience and comparison, can't be acquired by the amateur, semi-professional or professional who develops one, ten or twenty-five rolls of film once or twice a week. As a matter of fact, most processing technicians aren't even allowed out of the dimly lit labs for lunch, for fear daylight will ruin their eyes for the afternoon's work!

If you develop your film carefully, you should be able to produce an 8 x 10 print from either Plus-X or Tri-X which, even on glossy paper, is virtually grainless. In this size you shouldn't be able to distinguish any difference in quality between a shot made on Tri-X and one made on Plus-X. If you do see grain, if you can tell one film from the other in the 8 x 10 print, something is wrong with your developing technique or with your original exposure.

Improper processing causes graininess

The most frequent cause of so called grain is improper processing. All solutions must be kept within one or at the most two degrees of each other —this includes developer, fixer and wash water. A sudden change in temperature, even during the wash after processing is completed, can cause a loss in quality. (The picture doesn't actually become "grainy." The grains clump up and what you see is clumps of grain.) For top black-and-white results, don't overexpose. Overexposure causes an increase in grain size. Don't underexpose, for though graininess of the negative won't increase, the type of paper needed to print a thin negative tends to make graininess more apparent. And don't overdevelop. It's as bad as overexposure. And of course underdevelopment produces the same problem as underexposure. Again, watch those temperature variations!

There is one other factor concerning graininess which should be mentioned. *Modern Photography* magazine's Consulting Editor, John Wolbarst, who has probably done more practical research on 35mm film quality than any other technician, discovered an interesting phenomenon. When an image was sharp on the negative it appeared to be less grainy than when the same image was slightly out of focus. Apparently, when the viewer's eye sees a sharp image, the eye is satisfied with it. When the image is unsharp, the eye looks further and notices the grain.

I have no intention of carrying the processing of film and the making of prints any further. There are excellent volumes already written on each of these subjects alone and there is enough ground to cover in this book as it is.

Should you load your own film?

At this point I should like to say a word in defense of the very legitimate, money-saving, practice of bulk loading 35mm film. For ten years I have used up to 20 rolls of film a week, which could have put more than a slight dent in my bank balance if I had bought film in 20 or 36-exposure cartridges.

Both Plus-X Pan and Tri-X Pan are readily available in 100-ft. frame-numbered lengths. It's a simple matter to load your own cartridges, and I recommend it heartily. There are two bulk loaders currently available in the U.S. (They have been around for ten years or so and there doesn't seem to be reason to believe we'll see many others in the near future, although a couple of other interesting ones are available in Europe.) The inexpensive loader, the Lloyd, sells for about $5. It's made of plastic and consists of a light-tight chamber holding 100 ft. of film, a cartridge chamber and a felt-lip light trap through which the film is drawn into the cartridge chamber. You load the film into the chamber in the dark, then load each cartridge in roomlight. It's quite safe to do so. You disassemble a cartridge, attach the end of the film to the spool of the cartridge, reassemble the cartridge, place it in the cartridge chamber, shut the door and, with the handle provided, wind the film the appropriate number of times, as engraved on the loader lid. Then you open the cartridge chamber, cut the film, remove the cartridge and start on the next one.

It usually takes about a half hour to 45 minutes to load 18 36-exposure cartridges from a roll of 100 ft. My savings over store-bought film for this number of cartridges is enormous.

The Watson Loader, which costs about $12, has no felt light trap but, after the film is loaded, actually opens inside so the film touches nothing except the felt lip of the cartridge itself. It also has a built-in frame counter. While I think it's a fine device, I find the extra time needed to open and shut the interior light trap between film rolls, and the rather time-consuming method of getting cartridges in and out, overcomplicated and tedious. I have used the Lloyd tank with no scratches on my film, and have learned to count 31 turns (equal to 36 exposures) even while discussing religion and politics. Occasionally, between film loads, I give the Lloyd a dusting and clean the felt trap. It's a fine device and I recommend it.

There are special, and expensive cartridges made for reloading. I have never found any need for them. If you buy your film at first in factory-finished cartridges, handle them carefully while shooting they can be reused with no danger. I have settled on the Eastman Kodak or Ansco film cartridges as being quite adequate for reloading. The German Adox cartridges are really

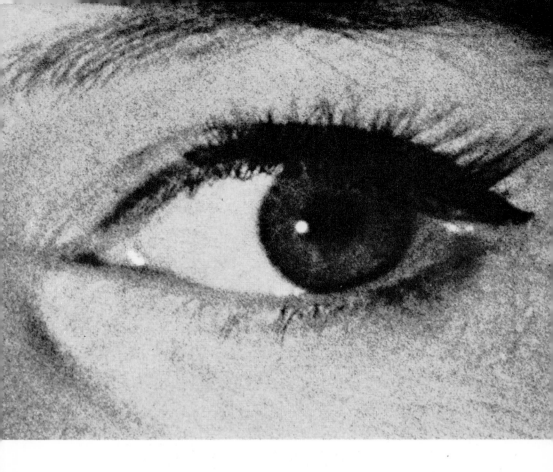

well built, perhaps the best available, and they're also easy to take apart. Eastman and Ansco cartridges are not. But if you can find a 25¢ Ekco "Lid Flipper" (a masterful jar-opener) at a supermarket or hardware store, you can open cartridges without fraying your temper or your fingernails.

Study the way Eastman Kodak fastens the film end to the central spool, and do likewise. Although you won't be able to use the splendid gooey tape that Kodak employs, cellophane or masking tape works nicely. Make sure you fasten the film end evenly so that the film will wind evenly. There should be little pressure as you begin turning the loader crank. If you feel resistance, stop and examine the cartridge and fastening.

It's advisable for the sake of economy to make 36- rather than 20-exposure loads. The smaller loads still need leaders and ends which will not be used. Naturally, the 36-exposure film requires less such wastage.

Don't try to save more by buying bargains in bulk film. Buy only factory-packed film specifically made for 35mm still photography. Both Plus-X and Tri-X are so available. The film can should bear an expiration date at least one year from the date you purchase the film.

There are few things as satisfactory in life as seeing a color picture you have taken projected in all its brilliance on a good-sized screen. It is so satisfying that many photographers never get around to shooting any black-

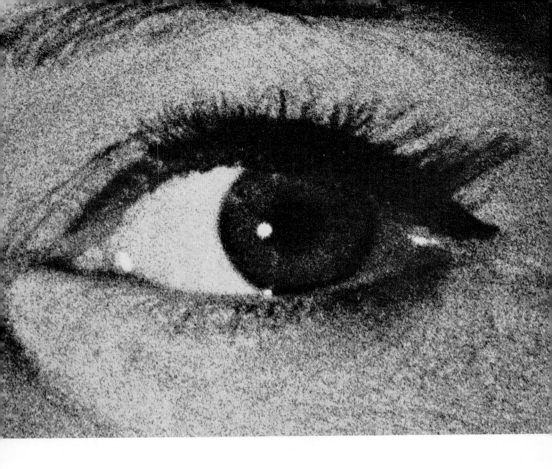

Do you really want fine grain?: At first glance the 75X blowup *at left* of the eye as outlined right does look sharper than the identical blowup *above*. But is the fine grain enlargement really sharper? Prop up the open book on a table and stand about 5 ft. away. Look again. Now which seems sharper. Surprised? Don't be. This is merely a primitive illustration to show that fine grain and sharpness are not the same, but that sharpness is actually the more important characteristic. According to researchers, it's the larger contrast areas (such as the point where the iris meets the white of the eye) which determine sharpness. Fine detail such as the delineation of the individual eyelashes is far less important. Picture *at left* was made from negative developed in fine grain developer. Negative used above was processed in Kodak D-76. Both pictures made on Kodak Panatomic-X.

and-white at all. Personally, I can't say that I prefer color over black and white, or vice-versa. I think of them as co-existing, offering different advantages, holding separate challenges. When you've been hard at work on one, the other comes as a pleasant relief.

If I were to state that the single-lens reflex offers a completely different technical approach to color, with different problems, I'd be untruthful. The problems of dealing with color itself are the same with one camera type or the other. And rather than go into a full-dress treatment of color here, I'd rather point out a few guideposts which you could follow in your own color work that you might not find elsewhere.

At present there are two types of color film available: negative transparency film from which prints or transparencies can be made, and transparency film from which prints can be made. At this stage of the game, transparency films (Kodachrome, Anscochrome, etc.) are far ahead in brilliance, color rendition, sharpness. Also, you have the transparency to view as soon as it's processed. With negative film you must have the finished negative printed before you have anything that you'd want to write home about. And transparencies made from it are not as satisfactory as those made from the best straight transparency film. Color prints from both nega-

Films are getting sharper too: In line with what you're just seen on the preceeding pages, film manufacturers have been increasing the sharpness of their new films without necessarily decreasing graininess. Above *left* is an enlarged section (75X again) made from the relatively new Kodak Tri-X Pan (improved type). Directly above is an equal enlargement from the same scene but made on the older Kodak Tri-X. Both films have the same ASA exposure index, and the graininess seems equal. If you step back a few feet however, you'll see that the enlargement from the new film looks sharper. Apparently the edge sharpness of each grain is more pronounced in the new film. Conclusions: Don't depend on finest grain films for sharpest pictures. For more punch use medium-speed films, fairly energetic developers.

LIGHT → / FILM ▼

Light	ANSCOCHROME (Daylight Type) Filter	E.I.	EKTACHROME E-2 Filter	E.I.	HIGH SPEED EKTACHROME Filter	E.I.	KODACHROME Filter	E.I.	SUPER ANSCOCHROME Filter	E.I.	TYPE F EKTACHROME Filter	E.I.
Fluorescents — Cool White	10B+30C	16	N.R.	N.R.	N.R.	N.R.	N.R.	N.R.	10B+30C	50	30M+20Y	12
Fluorescents — Warm White	20B+30C	16	N.R.	N.R.	N.R.	N.R.	N.R.	N.R.	20B+30C	50	20M+10Y	16
Fluorescents — White	20B+20C	16	N.R.	N.R.	N.R.	N.R.	N.R.	N.R.	20B+20C	50	20M+10Y	16
Fluorescents — Daylight	10B	25	20R	20	20R	100	20R	6	10B	80	N.R.	N.R.
Amber Flash (Dura, Solar—3200K)	N.R.	N.R.	N.R.	N.R.	N.R.	N.R.	N.R.	N.R.	N.R.	N.R.	N.R.	N.R.
Studio Floods (3200K)	80B+82A	8	80B+82A	8	See text	See text	80B+82A	3	80B+82A	25	82C	12
SM, SF Flash (3300K)	N.R.	N.R.	N.R.	N.R.	N.R.	N.R.	N.R.	N.R.	N.R.	N.R.	82B	50*
Photofloods (3400K)	80B	12	80B	12	See text	See text	80B	5	80B	40	82A	16
Clear Wire-Filled Flash (3800K)	N.R.	N.R.	80C	80*	80C	200*	80C	50*	N.R.	N.R.	None	120*
Blue Flashbulbs	None	95*	None	55*	None	200*	None	50*	None	170*	N.R.	N.R.
Electronic Flash	81A	32	None	32	None	160	None	10	81A	100	N.R.	N.R.
Late P.M. or Early A.M. Sunlight—Reddish	82A	25	82A	25	82A	125	82A	8	82A	80	85C	16
Open Shade, Marine, Cloudy, Distant Scenes	1A	32	1A	32	1A	160	1A	10	1A	100	85C	16
Sunlight plus Skylight—Average	None	32	None	32	None	160	None	10	None	100	85C	16

Color film filter and exposure index table (no textual column headers are printed; columns C1–C14 represent the unlabeled light‑source columns as read left to right).

Film		C1	C2	C3	C4	C5	C6	C7	C8	C9	C10	C11	C12	C13	C14
TYPE A															
KODACHROME	Filter	85C	85C	85C	85C	N.R.	None	82A	82B	82C	N.R.	N.R.	20M+10Y	20M+10Y	30M+20Y
	E.I.	10	10	10	10	N.R.	95*	12	40*	10	N.R.	N.R.	10	10	8
ANSCOCHROME TUNGSTEN (3400K) TYPE 532 A	Filter	85	85	85	N.R.	N.R.	81C	None	N.R.	82A	None	50R+50Y	20R+20Y	10R+20Y	40R+30Y
	E.I.	25	25	25	N.R.	N.R.	110*	32	N.R.	25	132*	12	16	16	12
KODACHROME PROFESSIONAL TYPE A	Filter	85	85	85	N.R.	N.R.	81C	None	None	82A	None	N.R.	30M+10Y	30M	30M+40Y
	E.I.	10	10	10	N.R.	N.R.	80*	16	50*	12	85*	N.R.	8	8	6
TYPE B															
HIGH SPEED EKTACHROME TYPE B	Filter	85B	85B	85B	85B	N.R.	81C	81A	81A	None	None	85B+30M+30Y	20M+20Y	20M+20Y	40M+50Y
	E.I.	80	80	80	80	N.R.	240*	100	120*	125	270*	64	80	80	40
SUPER ANSCOCHROME TUNGSTEN	Filter	85B	85B	85B	N.R.	N.R.	81D	81A	N.R.	None	None	50R+50Y	20R+20Y	10R+20Y	40R+30Y
	E.I.	80	80	80	N.R.	N.R.	220*	100	N.R.	100	230*	40	50	50	40
NEGATIVE															
AGFACOLOR CN14	Filter	None	1A	82A	85	N.R.	None	82A	N.R.	82C	N.R.	N.R.	20M+10Y	20M+10Y	30M+20Y
	E.I.	20	20	16	8	N.R.	90*	16	N.R.	12	N.R.	N.R.	10	10	8
AGFACOLOR CN17	Filter	None	1A	82A	85	N.R.	None	82A	82B	82C	N.R.	N.R.	20M+10Y	20M+10Y	20M+10Y
	E.I.	40	40	32	16	N.R.	140*	32	55*	20	N.R.	N.R.	20	20	16
KODACOLOR	Filter	None	1A	82A	85	N.R.	None	82A	82B	82C	N.R.	N.R.	20M+10Y	20M+10Y	30M+20Y
	E.I.	32	32	25	12	N.R.	120*	20	50*	16	N.R.	N.R.	16	16	12

Exposure indexes recommended for electronic flash are for use with guide number method of computing exposure. For High Speed Ektachrome, try these filters and indexes: Photofloods: 78A, E.I. 32; Studio floods: 78A + 82A, E.I. 20. Filtration for Kodachrome II with daylight 25 and tungsten 40 indexes are as given. However, guide and other exposure indexes have not been computed.

tive and positive transparency films are now about equal in quality. The best that can be said of negative films today is that they have an excellent future. The two leaders, Kodacolor and Agfacolor, do produce passable color prints and once in a while they border on the excellent. You can use the negatives to make fine black-and-white prints (particularly Agfacolor, which is virtually grainless). There are negative color films which can withstand slight errors in exposure; the errors can be corrected in printing. You can shoot them under many lighting conditions and the processor will balance the color properly during printing. But all color films are in competition with one of the photographic marvels of the ages. Its name is Kodachrome.

Kodachrome is best color film

Since 1936, when it was introduced, nothing has come near equalling the brilliance, sharpness and grainlessness of Kodachrome. Kodachrome is the standard by which all other color films are judged, consciously or unconsciously.

Why, then, are there so many other transparency films? The main reason is probably the extremely slow film speed of Kodachrome. At E.I. 10 (or the new 25) you need a great amount of light to expose it properly. If you're using floods, you must use big ones; if you are using electronic flash, you need a fairly powerful unit when you're any distance from your subject. Ergo, we have Anscochrome (E.I. 32), Super Anscochrome (E.I. 100), Ektachrome (E.I. 32), and High Speed Ektachrome (E.I. 160). And each of these films has one or more variations balanced for flash or floodlamps. After using many of these films over the years, I suggest that you use Kodachrome whenever you can. When there isn't enough light, use either Super Anscochrome or High Speed Ektachrome. Where light is poor, High Speed Ektachrome is excellent.

Exposing for color, I find, is tricky. Even Anscochrome has little latitude in comparison to black-and-white film. Make a mistake and that's it. Since any scene on a bright day has a tremendous range of varying brilliances, it's not surprising that most photographers wield their exposure meters in an absolute quandary. After years of listening to photographers tell me to expose for the highlights and forget about the shadow areas, expose for the shadows and let the highlights go, expose for the middle tones and let both highlight and shadow areas go, I evolved my own system, which works— for me. If a person's bright clothing is slightly overexposed and thus washed out, your eye may not notice. If shadows are underexposed and have little or no detail, this is also forgivable. But if flesh tones aren't natural, your viewing eye will notice it and be disturbed. I expose all color in which flesh tones are important by taking a close-up reading for the flesh tones. It doesn't fail. If the skin is light, it registers correctly. If it's a Negro or Arabic skin, it captures all the richness and detail in it. Most of the time I'm quite satisfied with the colors of the surrounding area and clothing. But if something has to yield slightly, it must be those. I'll keep my facial tones, thank you.

When shooting unpeopled scenics or scenics in which people play a minor role, there's no sense in reading for flesh tones. Read for a middle tone instead. For the most accuracy, hold an 18 percent reflectance grey card (available from your photo dealer) under the same lighting as the most important area of your picture. I confess, however, to an aversion for toting a large grey card with me. Instead, I generally substitute the palm of my hand which, while not an 18 percent grey, seems to be workably adequate (picture, page 38). For special situations—distance scenes, backlit scenes, silhouettes—consult the instruction booklet that comes with your meter. Our recommended meters, Weston Master and General Electric, both have excellent instruction booklets.

Most picture-taking under daylight conditions will give you little trouble as far as good overall color balance is concerned (use a Skylight 1A filter if you find your color coming out a little too blue for your taste), but moving indoors and using flood, flash and other forms of tungsten illumination can tie you into knots. Unfortunately there is no place you can go for comprehensive information on which filters must be used for what film, so, although I've done my best to keep confusing charts out of this book, I do feel in this case that giving you a comprehensive film and filter listing as compiled by Norman Rothschild (pages 46 and 47) will be of service.

No chapter on exposure could be called complete without some angry words on the subject of the flash, both bulb and electronic. For direct flash from camera position, an ugly light for most subjects, follow the guide numbers of the flashbulb manufacturers. Most electronic flash guide numbers furnished by manufacturers are at least one full f/stop greater than they ought to be. In any case, never use any type of flash until you have tested the bulb or unit out with the type of film you intend to use beforehand. If you like the soft even qualities of bounce flash, use about two lens openings larger than the direct flash guide number indicates if you're bouncing from an average 10-foot white ceiling. Open up or shut down further if the ceiling is higher or lower.

After exposure, proper processing is essential. Almost all amateurs and even professionals today have color film processed for them. I have discovered that processing can vary wildly from one processor to another. Often I've blamed the poor film manufacturer for errors really committed by the processor. I've found over the years that it is well worth the extra time to send color film through the photo dealer back to the film manufacturer for processing. By and large, the manufacturers are the most consistent and reliable, if the most expensive and the slowest. When you do find a good processor, stick with him, encourage him and tell your friends about him. He deserves all the praise and business he can get.

You can save money by buying bulk color film, just as you can with black-and-white, but beware of respooled movie film, of aerial film, of government surplus color film. Make sure you buy factory-packed film made especially for 35mm still cameras. And don't fall into one of the traps which offers bulk film and respooled bulk film at attractive prices which include the cost of processing. Maybe the film's O.K. Maybe the processing is all right. Maybe the first order you send in turns out nicely. What guarantee have you that you'll get the same film and processing the second time around? Generally you won't get that far. The initial results will probably lead you back to the legitimate channels for obtaining color film.

It beats me why so many photographers will spend money on good cameras and then feed junk through them.

4

THE

TRUTH

ABOUT

LENSES

The number of different lenses available for eye-level reflexes is fantastic. There are upwards of 500 ranging in focal length from 21 to 1000mm and from a few dollars to many thousands.

With such a surfeit or glut, depending on how you look at it, in a field where the price of a 135mm f/3.5 lens can vary from $24.95 to $200, a cold, dispassionate, practical look at the lenses themselves is absolutely necessary.

First, some truths about all lenses for prism reflexes:

1. No two lenses, even if the same aperture, the same focal length and the same make, are exactly alike in performance.

2. The best camera and lens makers, while producing the best lenses, also let a number of "dogs" get by (in error, we hope).

3. While no lens is perfect, some few lenses are capable of astounding performance.

4. A company which produces one astounding lens is quite capable of making another which is equally as bad as the first is good.

5. Almost no lens made for single-lens reflexes delivers its best performance at full opening. Almost all produce better results at f/5.6 and f/8.

6. The quality of lenses can only be discussed in comparison with other lenses since there is no practical-to-use standard of optical perfection.

Lens quality is an important, complex, misunderstood, fascinating, difficult-to-comprehend subject.

What do we mean by lens quality? Sharpness is certainly important, but is not the whole problem by a long shot. But what, indeed, is sharpness and how can it be defined? I was fairly sure until recently when someone took issue with my statement that a specific lens lacked good sharpness and sent me in some pocket-sized snapshots to prove how good the lens in question was.

For him, a lens which produces sharpness in a wallet-size picture is sharp. Here's the other end of the scale: I was asked recently what 35mm camera lens might produce absolutely sharp 16 x 20 enlargements which could be inspected with a magnifying glass. In this test, no 35mm camera lens in general use today could be called a sharp lens.

Here then is my standard of sharpness. It is in line with what a critical professional photographer who depends on sharp pictures for a living should expect from his camera and lens.

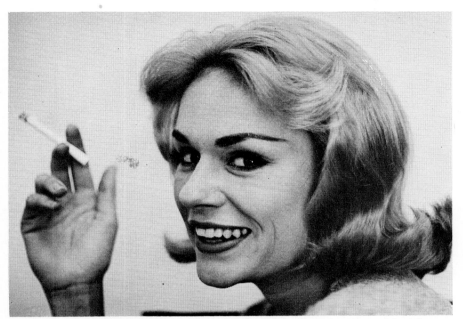

Big lens mystery: Both pictures were made with a famous 58mm f/1.4 lens at maximum aperture. In the top picture the girl is in focus but her hand which is on the same plane as her face, is out of focus. Now, to make matters . . .

. . . more confusing, in this picture again made at f/1.4, the girl has moved her hand slightly forward, but now her hand is sharper! You can control this phenomenon only with a reflex. Read this chapter to find out why and how.

To check camera alignment: Tack newspaper to wall. Draw heavy pencil line down one sheet. Place camera at 45° to paper about 20 inches from line. Shoot wide open focused at line. Develop film and examine for results.

A fine-grain film negative from a top lens when enlarged to 11 x 14 should at all apertures produce sharpness from corner to corner which approaches that produced centrally at f/5.6 by a top-brand lens. The closer the approach, the better the lens.

This may seem a peculiar method of determining lens sharpness, but actually it's extremely practical. Every normal focal length lens as supplied on an eye-level reflex today produces near to excellent quality at the center when used at f/5.6. Since everyone reading this book who owns such a camera can produce or have made such a print showing this sharpness, you have an immediate basis for comparing not only the performance of other lenses you might buy, but of the actual lens you're using as a control as well. Just compare the sharpness at any aperture with central definition at f/5.6 (see illustrations, pages 54 and 55).

Here's a very uncomplicated practical method I've evolved for testing lens sharpness. First test camera alignment (see pictures, pages above). If a camera is in alignment, focus on the ground glass must be exactly the same as focus on the film plane.

1. Using masking tape, tack a piece of newspaper with fine print (classified advertising will do) on a wall and with a heavy grease pencil draw a straight vertical line down the middle of one sheet.

Correct alignment: Line is sharp with definition falling off before and behind it. Camera is properly aligned.

Bad alignment: Sharpest plane is off line. Camera must be taken to repairman for realignment.

2. Load your camera with Plus-X or any other fine or medium fine grain film.

3. With your camera on a tripod at approximately the height of the middle of the newspaper, place your camera to the side of the paper at an angle of about 45 degrees about 3 ft. from the paper.

4. Focus on the vertical line.

5. Using either daylight filtering into the room or artificial light, shoot a picture at maximum lens aperture.

6. With a magnifying glass, examine the negative. If the black line is sharp and definition falls off in front of it and behind it, the camera body itself is properly aligned. If some other plane is slightly sharper than the line, the interior mirror is not placed properly or there is some other misalignment. The camera must be aligned before any lens check can be made.

Now for the sharpness test.

1. Using a fine or medium grained film, place your camera on a tripod and focus at infinity a distant group of buildings or other subject matter with detail. There should be detail in the center and also at the picture corner. Cross lighting which brings out detail sharply is preferable.

2. With the camera locked rigidly in place shoot pictures at all apertures by varying the shutter speed to maintain constant exposure, determined

by a careful meter reading. Keep notes on apertures so you can identify the negatives later.

3. Develop the film according to the manufacturer's instructions. Pick out the f/5.6 negative and with a magnifier of at least 10X examine the central sharpness. Compare it with the sharpness at the edges. Compare the sharpness of all the other apertures as well.

If you have difficulty in distinguishing one sharpness from another, don't fret. It simply indicates that there isn't much difference.

Obviously a visual test as indicated is sketchy. For more precise comparison, enlargements must be made. Since making 11 x 14 enlargements of all apertures can run into money, here's what we suggest. Make or have made 11 x 14 glossy enlargements of the entire negative at maximum aperture, at f/2.8, f/5.6, and f/11. That's a maximum number of 4 enlargements. Use a good enlarger with a reputable enlarging lens stopped down to f/5.6. Focus carefully. Now you will have four enlargements which you can compare quickly side by side. If you've used a building or scene near your home you have the beginnings of a regular test series which you can run on any lens you wish at any time the weather is right. Always use the same film, the same developer and the same processing times to maintain uniformity.

How much unsharpness should you tolerate in a lens? It depends on the type of lens. In normal lenses there should be little difference between the sharpness at the center and the edges from f/2.8 to f/22. At f/1.9, f/2 or thereabouts, a small amount of fuzziness at the edges and a slight loss of sharpness in the center must be expected. With an f/1.1, 1.2, 1.4 or 1.5 lens,

IN 35MM LENSES, THE DIFFERENCE IS GREATER

A comparison between an under $40 average 35mm wide-angle lens and a more expensive good quality one shows a greater disparity in definition than was seen with 135mm lenses. While the central definition is noticeably sharper and better in the more expensive lens at full aperture, edge definition of the bargain lens remains quite poor even at the critical f/5.6 aperture. Obviously, a wide-angle lens at a low price is less of a bargain than a 135mm telephoto or long-focus lens—unless you run across the rare exception.

CENTER DEFINITION AT f/3.5

BARGAIN LENS▶

QUALITY LENS▶

edge definition may be slightly fuzzier but should not blur completely.

Tele or long focal length lenses: They should perform in a manner quite similar to the normal lens although a very fast tele lens may outperform a normal lens at a large aperture. A telephoto, although shorter in overall physical length and more complicated in optical design will perform just as well as a good long focal length lens.

Wide-angle lenses: Partly because these lenses represent very complicated optical design few if any wide-angle lenses perform with the definition of the normal and tele lenses. While the center of a wide-angle 35mm lens may be as sharp at f/5.6 as a normal lens, the edge definition will probably be less so. In shorter focal lengths—30 or 28mm—sharpness will be even less, particularly at the edges. With a 24mm lens, don't expect acceptable definition at the edges until you reach f/5.6. And definition will never be what you would call excellent at any aperture.

Actually, you pretty well get the sharpness you pay for. In recent years a great number of what seem to be sensational buys in lenses have appeared. The lenses generally bear strange names—Optinar, Fujita, Taika, Acall, Juplen, Sonnagor, etc. Most are Japanese, but not all.

Since I'm always in the market for a bargain, I've tested quite a number of lenses which sell for less than $50. Here's what you can expect from such lenses: *Telephoto*: Most are surprisingly good even at full (f/3.5 or f/2.8) aperture and centrally almost equal to the best at f/5.6 or smaller apertures. *Wide angle*: Bargain lenses show up poorly in short focal lengths with central definition at full opening barely passable and edge definition defi-

EDGE DEFINITION AT f/3.5   CENTER DEFINITION AT f/5.6   EDGE DEFINITION AT f/5.6

nitely not acceptable. At f/5.6, central definition improves but edge definition remains poor. (See illustrations, pages 54 and 55).

If you have a limited budget it would seem most practical to spend the large portion on the wide angle and, if you can, get a bargain in a telephoto.

Remember, however, that our terms are quite critical and will yield pictures to 11 x 14. If you are only interested in wallet-sized snapshots, you need not be so choosy.

Since many eye-level reflex owners shoot partly or wholly in color, you may wonder why I've been stressing black-and-white tests. It's difficult to judge the sharpness of a color transparency when projected. Color prints are never really sharp. Secondly, a poorly corrected lens will often yield an excellent transparency but poor black-and-white negatives. However, a lens which produces clean, sharp black-and-white negatives will virtually always produce excellent color. So, we test in black and white.

Use distant scene for sharpness test

Why test for sharpness on a distant scene rather than a medium close brick wall (which is often recommended) or by using one of the many test charts available? It's claimed that these test charts make child's play of comparing lenses. Just count the finest lines which appear on the negative and you have a definite number to assign to the performance of your lens.

Unfortunately most tests made in this manner can lead you into a serious misconception about good lenses as far as practical photography is concerned. A lens can be quite excellent in use and test poorly on a brick wall or testing chart.

Almost all lenses in use for 35mm cameras suffer from a fault known as curvature of field (diagram, page 58). At any given focusing distance, the objects in the center of the field will come to a focus on a different plane than the objects at the edges. If at f/1.4 to f/2 you focus your camera carefully at a two-dimensional close distance subject, the resulting negative or transparency may show the edges out of focus. Focus on the edge and the center may be unsharp. This inability of the lens to produce a flat two-dimensional image in focus from corner to corner is caused by the curvature of field. The actual plane of sharpness is a curve which can actually be plotted. This curvature can best be seen at close focusing distances where there is little depth of field to compensate for it. As a result, many people in testing lenses at close distances using a brick wall or test charts mistake the curvature of field for lens unsharpness (picture, page 58). Lenses with curvature of field may be sharp at full aperture but not on a single focusing plane. Our test at infinity indicated a lens' ability to produce a sharp image regardless of field curvature.

I've made this distinction between lack of sharpness and curvature of field for definite reasons. Unless you are actually shooting flat subjects at full aperture such as in copy work (which nobody does) the curvature of field will seldom if ever be sufficient to affect your pictures. At smaller apertures than f/2 the depth of field even at close distances compensates for the curvature and it is therefore undetectable.

What types of subject matter do you shoot at full apertures? Generally subjects in very low light where you must open your lens fully if you have any hope of getting a transparency or a printable negative. Seldom, if ever, are these subjects completely flat. Generally you are focusing on a central subject with other objects at the edges of the picture area, either nearer or slightly farther away, from the camera.

Obviously if you knew exactly in which direction your curvature of field extended, you could put it to use and get a sharper picture than if you had a lens with little or no curvature of field (pictures, page 51).

While most curvatures of field extend in a curve forward from the center of the field, it's best to make a rough test.

With your camera loaded with fine grained film, place it on a tripod and focus at 2-3 ft. on a brick wall making sure your camera is absolutely parallel to it. Shoot wide open with the lens in absolute center focus. Now turn the lens mount a tiny bit towards the infinity position and shoot another negative. Make six negatives, turning the lens each time slightly further towards infinity. Make notations as to how far you've turned each time. Now start over, but this time, turn the lens from the central point of sharpness towards its closest focusing distance. When you develop the film, a check with the magnifying glass will quickly tell you whether you have curvature of field and which way it extends. If the edges get sharper and the center becomes fuzzy in the negatives shot as you turned the mount towards infinity, your curvature extends backwards at the edges away from the lens. This is the usual curvature direction, most often found in high speed lenses. If the edges become sharper as you turned the lens towards its closest focusing point, curvature extends forwards at the edges, towards the camera.

Once you know in which direction your curvature extends, you can put it to some use. If the curvature extends backwards at the picture edges, you know that edge subject material slightly behind the central image will be sharper than subject material slightly in front of the main subject or vice-versa, and plan your pictures accordingly.

Most fast lenses have field curvature

I've delved into the intricacies of field curvature to a great extent because I've never seen it discussed adequately from a practical standpoint anywhere. I've met so many photographers—amateurs and professionals— who tested their lenses at close distances, found the edges fuzzy, and tossed the lens away. Since many of our very best normal speed lenses for eye-level reflexes such as the 58mm f/1.4 Nikkor, have such curvature of field, it's advisable to know what it is and how to use it.

Incidentally, curvature of field shows up in a much more pronounced manner with a reflex camera than with a rangefinder camera. Generally, in aligning a lens to a rangefinder, the manufacturer sets the lens not at the sharpest central point or at the edges but somewhere between, thus effecting a compromise. It is virtually impossible to get the sharpest central or edge definition when shooting wide open on a flat field. In a reflex, you can focus sharply at the center and see the lack of sharpness at the edges. By refocusing for the corners (if you have a full ground glass) you will see the center becoming unsharp. If you arrange your subjects you can get sharpness in the center and at the edges.

Besides curvature of field, there are three other tests everyone should

Horrors, definition falloff!: Don't throw your lens away if you photograph a brick wall closeup at maximum aperture and get this result. The lens may merely have curvature of field. However, the brick wall test is a splendid way of determining whether a lens does have field curvature *(see text).*

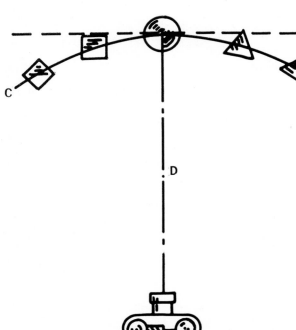

How to make the most from curvature: If your lens has field curvature (and the larger its maximum aperture, the greater the chances that it does) determine in which way it curves and make the most of it by arranging subject material properly (along C), when shooting at short distances, (D). That's how shots on page 51 were made. To get over-all sharpness for copying flat work, use small aperture and curvature will disappear.

perform with the lens that comes with his camera and any other lens he buys.

1. *Vignetting and shutter speed*: While testing for vignetting, you can do a shutter speed test for your camera at the same time. Outdoors, point your camera at a clear blue sky, or indoors, at a white wall, cardboard, or piece of paper which is evenly illuminated. Make a series of exposures at all shutter speeds and apertures, varying the speeds and apertures to maintain the same exposure. When you have your film developed, examine the negatives. All should be even in density. If some are darker, overall, than others, your shutter speeds are erratic and should be fixed (see pictures, page 60). If one edge of a frame is darker than another that particular shutter speed has faulty focal plane curtain travel. This generally occurs at the fastest speeds—$\frac{1}{500}$, $\frac{1}{1000}$ sec. Now, vignetting: Some lenses at full opening do not transmit as much light to the negative edges as they do to the center. This causes a hot spot in the center of the picture area with a loss of light at the edges (see picture, page 61). Vignetting can also be caused by the lens barrel or the camera lens mount itself. The mount opening and barrel may be insufficiently large to allow the edges of the picture to receive enough illumination. Both types of vignetting will appear on the negatives as a lightening at the negative edges.

2. *Barrel and pincushion distortion*: Photograph a flat subject with horizontal and vertical lines such as a brick wall. Are the lines straight or do they curve? Lines curving inwards at the center indicate pincushion distortion. Lines curving outwards indicate barrel distortion. Such distortions are most common in zoom lenses (diagram, page 61). Obviously such a lens is unsuitable for any kind of photography in which perpendicular or horizontal lines are important as in copy work or architectural photography.

Lens mounts also differ

Optics isn't the only point to check when buying a lens. The more expensive ones usually have smoother, more rigid and longer-lasting lens mounts. The lenses that are less expensive generally have softer threads whose tolerances are not as fine as the better lenses. If you will be giving your accessory lenses real workouts, good ones may be worth your while for a better lens mount alone.

Examine the focusing mounts of lenses carefully. Some lenses have astonishingly close focusing mounts which are extremely handy for taking portraits and close-ups. Recently I was pleased to find that the 100mm f/2 Super Canomatic for the Canonflex focused down to 3½ ft.—far closer than the 105mm f/2.5 Nikkor on the Nikon F or the 100mm Auto-Rokkor on the Minolta Reflex. If such a feature is important to your work, examine any lens you buy carefully and check the close focusing ability of alternative lenses as well.

Maximum aperture is another extremely important feature. Obviously, the wider the maximum aperture the lower the light level in which you can shoot. But the larger maximum apertures also make focusing easier by providing a more brilliant prism image and also by narrowing the depth of field at full aperture. This has effect of making the image move in and out of focus more sharply and swiftly.

Shutter speed test: It matters little if the shutter speeds are slightly off (and only a technician can test for it) but shutter speeds should be consistent. Varying aperture to maintain constant exposure, shoot a blank sky at all shutter speeds. Resulting frames should be exactly alike in density.

Examine the focusing mount for one last feature—the amount of turn necessary to change the mount from its nearest focusing distance to infinity.

Some lenses can move only a quarter of a turn. They are relatively easy to focus and excellent where speed is essential, such as in sports photography. Other mounts must be turned a full 360 degrees. These may be more precise in their focusing but appear more difficult to focus because they change focus more slowly for any given turn of the mount. I know of one 400mm lens which takes four whole turns to move from 22 ft. to infinity!

Leaf-shutter camera lens mounts

The owner of a leaf-shutter single-lens reflex with interchangeable front element components or complete interchangeability may feel left out by our foregoing discussion since such cameras are limited to the lenses provided by the camera manufacturer. The lenses for these cameras range from 28mm to 135mm. The maximum apertures are generally rather small. The close focusing distances are sometimes overly long—in one case, 14 ft. for a 135mm lens, making it absolutely unusable for portrait photography unless a close-up lens is attached to the 135mm lens.

The longer focal length lenses for these leaf-shutter reflexes, however, tend to be slightly better in overall performance than the wide angle. None of the accessory lenses will be as good as the normal focal length lens because of the many optical problems which must be overcome in designing lenses for these cameras.

Vignetting: Here's a classic example of a lens not able to cover the picture area properly. Not only are the edges unsharp but they are dark as well, indicating that the corners are not receiving sufficient illumination. The lens, a 250mm telephoto, is definitely inadequate at this aperture on this camera.

Barrel and pincushion: If straight lines in your picture curve inwards (pincushion) or outwards (barrel) the lens has a defect which will show up at all apertures, particularly when straight-line subject material appears at the picture edges. Zoom lenses often suffer from this distortion.

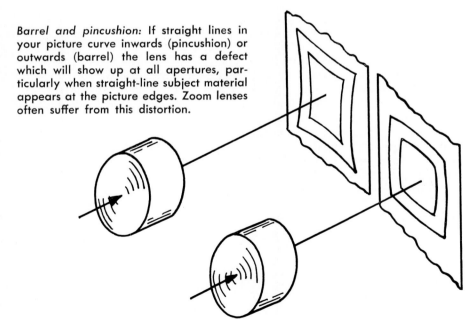

If you own a leaf-shutter reflex and wish an extremely long lens, beyond the 135mm length, you are in luck. The monoculars (half a binocular) which are now being made primarily for photographic use are almost universally of good quality. They fit directly over the front of the regular camera lens and are generally held in place by regular filter adapter rings. In spite of their small physical length and light weight, they are extremely powerful. To calculate the effective focal length simply multiply the power of the monocular by the focal length of the normal lens (for instance an 8X monocular used with a 50mm lens would produce an 8 x 50 or 400mm focal length lens). Maximum apertures however, are generally limited to about f/14. These monoculars are subject to some barrel or pincushion distortion.

With the advent of the zoom lens an entirely new area is opening up for the single-lens reflex, both leaf-and focal-plane shuttered. Since it's almost a necessity to have a through-the-lens viewfinder, the zoom lens will probably be designed exclusively for single-lens reflex cameras.

How good are zoom lenses?

Today there are but a few zoom lenses. These are rather large and bulky, and expensive. The zoom lenses covering the shorter focal lengths, from wide angle to medium telephotos are rather unsharp, especially at wide apertures. The longer focal length zoom lenses are sharper. It will be some time however before these lenses which often incorporate as many as fifteen glass elements will be practical and inexpensive enough for the average photographer. The potential is enormous, since it will be possible to fit the focal length instantly to whatever subject and situation you are facing. In addition, the single-lens reflex prism finder will show you just what's happening through the lens every moment you're using it.

At the opposite end of the price scale are the new small aperture long focal length lenses. Led by the Encino Engineering Co. of California, a number of firms are now manufacturing 400mm lenses of limited apertures—f/7.5, f/6.9—for single-lens reflexes. These very light lenses which make use of optics generally reserved for telescopes are quite inexpensive, relatively speaking. Many, particularly the f/7.5 lenses, are fantastically sharp. Outdoors, using a reasonably fast film, there's no reason why they can't be hand held.

There is one variety of lens attachment which I must warn you to avoid. The auxiliary wide angle and tele attachments which fit in front of your normal camera lens (except for the monocular already discussed) are too poor in quality to consider for anything but the smallest of snapshots.

The subject of lenses is quite endless and one can write an entire series of books on optics alone (it's been done, too). However, we've covered the major points that you should know.

Coating: amber or blue?

You will probably hear or become involved in arguments on amber vs. blue lens coating, the necessity of half stops, seven-element vs. six element designs, flare, coma, contrast, etc., etc. All of these points do have some validity but the sum of all added together constitutes more talk and testing than practical photography.

And if your lens has air bubbles? Then it has air bubbles along with thousands of other excellent lenses whose reputations were assured until some manufacturer decided that he would imply that lenses without bubbles were far better. As a matter of fact, his lenses now have bubbles too. So do most of mine.

5

WHAT
LENS,
WHERE
AND
HOW?

The interchangeable lens today is an integral part of an eye-level reflex photographer's necessary equipment. It's no longer just an expensive toy. Modern lens designs and light alloy mounts have brought cost, weight and size to a point where every serious photographer—amateur or professional —considers tele and wide-angle lenses absolute necessities.

Tele and wide-angle lenses still have narrow, rigid uses for some photographers. A telephoto brings objects closer, a wide-angle lens pushes them farther away. He uses one only when he can't approach close enough to his subject and the other when he couldn't back away far enough.

But changes in focal length not only alter apparent camera-to-subject distance, but produce entirely different apparent perspective. We change lenses to show an old subject in a new way, to emphasize some part of a subject and minimize others, to suit the mood of the subject and our own, to allow the picture viewers see things as we want them to.

The pictures on pages 66 and 67 were made with lenses from 21 to 1000mm, from a fixed camera-to-subject distance. By comparing each with that made by the 50mm lens you'll see exactly how the areas covered by each lens differ.

For landscapes, the wide-angle lens is excellent. You've seen the group portraits of a man surrounded by the sculpture he makes or the paintings he collects. Here, too, the wideangle lens with its ability to cover a greater area than the normal lens used at the same subject-to-camera distance proves its worth. In recent years, we've expanded the use of the lens even further by learning to use effectively the apparent distortions which such lenses can produce (see page 71).

Probably the most common apparent distortion caused by wide-angle lenses is the building falling over backward. It's apparent distortion because

Use a long lens: The children were racing to the edge of a float and jumping into the water some hundreds of yards offshore, I was on shore. Instead of wading over my head, camera in hand, or turning into a submarine, I fastened a 400mm f/7.5 Astronar lens to the Minolta SR-2 and comfortably blazed away from shore for about half an hour. I admit that the children noticed me and the lens (the lens is rather long and difficult to hide underneath a coat) and redoubled their efforts. Will 1/500 sec. stop most action? You bet it will.

21mm

28mm

55mm

105mm

250mm

500mm

this common picture is not the fault of the lens. If you look up at a building and assume that your eyes are really looking straight ahead, what's the building doing? Falling over backward. Actual distortion occurs only when there are faults in the lens itself. All lenses will perform this trick to some degree if you point your camera upward. Wide-angle lenses, however, show more of the building (and so, more of the lean). And since you're probably closer to the building with the wide-angle lens, you point the camera upward at an even steeper angle, and so the building leans and leans and leans. The correction of the lean is simple. Keep the film plane parallel to the building. Don't point it upward or downward. You can't get the whole building into the picture? Get farther away. Photographers also noticed, in using a wide-angle lens, that hands or noses or anything else thrust close to the lens

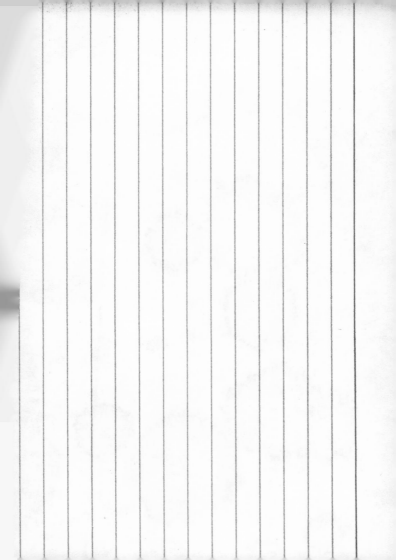

35mm

50mm

135mm

180mm

1000mm

How do different focal lengths compare in their ability to cover specific areas? This series was taken with the Nikkor lenses for the Nikon F Reflex from the widest lens available, the 21mm, to the longest, a 1000mm which employs mirror optics.

appeared enormous in relation to the rest of the picture (see pictures, page 70). Here, too, the distortion is apparent, not real. The rules for proper viewing of prints state that your eye should be no farther from the picture than the focal length of the lens multiplied by the degree of enlargement of the picture. If you look at the picture of the girl and ice cream stick (page 70) from about six inches, you'll see that the shot looks quite natural. An ice cream stick held close to your eye *would* look big.

If pointing a camera upward makes a building lean and a wide-angle lens accentuates the effect, use it to show all subjects from new angles to make them more exciting. But be prepared for the results. If objects close to the wide-angle lens increase in size, use this for interesting effects (see picture, page 71). In addition, enlarged size connotes power. Horses, when

Apparent distortion with wide angle: A wide angle lens' apparent perspective distortion can be used effectively for hilarious results. Here, a 28mm f/3.5 Angenieux lens on an Exakta VX camera records a conversation between four pairs of feet. The camera was pointed downwards by the owner of the bottom feet and an exposure of about f/16 at a forgotten shutter speed produced the picture on Panatomic-X film.

Apparent distortion with tele: Besides the Caribbean natives' general mistrust of photographers, I had another reason for using a 135mm f/4 Carl Zeiss Triotar lens on my Exakta VX. The hilly street was rather long. The long focal length lens tended to compress the street (which was in Scarborough, Tobago) and made it seem more active than it actually was. Shooting at 1/250 sec. at f/11 with Panatomic-X film, I merely waited until the street became filled with an interesting group of people. A number of similar pictures were also made with different natives, both in color and black-and-white.

photographed from straight on, look powerful if their heads and shoulders are proportionately bigger than their flanks or the plow behind them. Trains appear more massive and fast if the locomotives or engines seem larger than the cars following. Use wide-angle lenses whenever you want to concentrate interest. A pair of hands holding magnifying glass and object being examined dominates a picture while the head and shoulders of the owner of the hands recedes into appropriate obscurity in the background.

What wide angle lens should you buy?

How wide an angle lens do you buy and what aperture should it be? For a first lens purchase a 28- or 35mm. Either is wide enough for you to shoot landscapes and try the apparent distortions, but not so wide as to land you in trouble.

Trouble with wide-angle lenses? The wider the lens, the more the apparent distortion gets out of hand. For instance, with a 21mm lens, the slightest tilt from a plane absolutely parallel to the subject will produce an amazing amount of apparent distortion. Subjects close to the edges of the picture area start to look flat and distended (center picture, above). Camera-to-subject distance must be great or your foreground-to-background distance seems tremendously exaggerated.

Far left: Perhaps the exaggeration is rather great but you can see how any foreground object will look overly large in comparison to the rest of the subject when shooting with a wide-angle lens at a close distance.

Center: Subjects close to the corners or edges of the picture area will look flattened out and distorted when shot with a wide-angle lens.

Right: Here Frank Wolfe, who made these functional shots, uses the wide angle lens' apparent distortion effectively. Rather than avoid the apparent distortion produced by such lenses, think how you can make it work for you instead.

There are many interesting extreme wide-angle scenes that can be shot with a 21mm lens. But you'll find more uses for a 35 or 28mm lens.

Why more long lenses are being used

There is a definite trend to the longer focal lengths today. Ten years ago a tele or long focal length lens, even among the professionals, generally meant a 90- or 135mm. The 90mm was used mostly for portraits. You could shoot a good head and shoulders portrait with little chance that apparent distortion would make arms, hands or noses look larger than they should. The 135mm was used principally for making big images from distant subjects. Then a shift began. The 135mm began to be used for portraits. The longer focal length lens at wide aperture could pick a subject out of his surroundings, and the limited depth of field when shooting fairly close to a subject isolated the person from the background, no matter how confusing or complicated it was. Photographers who simply didn't have the time (or often the inclination) to ask a subject to move, shot the victim where he stood. By moving back even farther with the 135mm, photographers tried the lens for head-to-toe portraits where they wished to bring the background close behind the subject (the beautifully grained wood office wall behind the architect, for instance).

Anyone for the decisive moment? While both these pictures are actually from the same series as the photograph on page 54, I simply couldn't resist illustrating the ease with which you can follow action and shoot at precisely the right moment, provided you have a single lens reflex to go with your 400mm lens. Of course, you must anticipate slightly—press the release just as the little girl leaves from the float and just as her hands start to break water. You and I may misjudge more than occasionally, but what pictures we can get when we anticipate correctly!

Except for the need to hold a long lens extremely steady (try thinking of it as target practice with a precision rifle), there's little optical trouble in store for you. The only apparent distortion, of course, is the shortening of distances in depth (called foreshortening) which makes subject matter appear jammed together (picture, page 68). Sometimes, as on a crowded beach, this foreshortening can make your picture more interesting. If you want to show people on just one distance plane, just open up your lens and objects at distances other than the one at which you are focused will be so unsharp at f/3.5 or f/2.8 you won't even notice them.

Lenses over 135mm for portraits?

It wasn't too long before photographers began casting about for something a trifle longer. The new portrait lens for many today is the 180mm to 200mm. Light long lenses on eye-level reflex cameras can be hand-held even at ⅛₀ sec. A crowded room becomes a virtual sea of faces from which you pick and choose with a 180mm lens. With narrow extension tubes between the lens and camera body you can focus a long lens closer than its normal close focusing distance. No week seems to go by these days without some

Congressional inquiry in Washington being seen in *Life* magazine through giant, extreme close-ups of the witnesses, the congressmen or senators and the investigators. How are they done? With 180mm lenses.

When photographers reach the 180mm level, they begin to wonder just how long a lens they can hand-hold and still keep steady. Today, a 300- to 400mm lens is not unusual. Even advanced amateurs and semi-professionals are using them. These lenses are a trifle too long for portraiture. However, until you've gone hunting birds or people with a 300mm hand-held lens you haven't really learned how exciting interchangeable lenses can make photography.

Over 400mm, use a tripod always

How about the lenses longer than 400mm? You'll have to go back to a tripod. The lenses of 500-, 600-, 800mm and upwards are not for hand holding. In experiments I found lenses up to 800mm not too hard to use provided you own a really steady heavy tripod. At 1000- and 2000mm, troubles began. The slightest breeze causes enough camera and lens movement to blur the picture. A tiny bit of haze, even on a brilliant day, makes sharp pictures difficult. At 2000mm, heat waves and air turbulence which you can't even see make the lenses almost impossible to use. Objects seemed to undulate like flags when seen through the waves of heat rising from the ground between the lens and the object.

In the longer focal lengths, 1000- and 2000mm, you have your choice of either straight glass optics or mirror optics. The mirror lenses are much like the large reflecting telescopes used at the larger astronomical observatories. Using mirrors instead of glass, their physical size has been reduced considerably. The regular lens, at 1000- or 2000mm is impressively long and rather cumbersome. Optically, the two types are about equal in quality.

Among the most recent lens developments for single lens reflex cameras are the Bushnell Spacemaster and the zoom lenses.

Telescope and zoom lenses

The Spacemaster is quite a spectacular small sporting telescope much like many other small telescopes except that it is fitted for attaching to a single lens reflex camera. Using this small unit you can have the equivalent of anything from a 750- to 3000mm lens! The price of the unit is not great and the definition at the center of the field is good although the corners of the picture may be soft and dark. The lens also has some barrel and pincushion distortion (see page 61) and the maximum apertures are relatively small, f/50 at 3000mm. However, with today's extremely fast films even this small opening should be sufficient for most outdoor pictures. You will need a very sturdy tripod to use it, however.

Although three zoom lenses are now available, the zoom lens is more of a development to watch in the future than to consider now. Undoubtedly, the still reflex cameras will turn to zoom lenses in the same manner that movie cameras did—when the lenses are less expensive, small and of good quality. The possibilities, including following the action in a football game from one sideline to the other while standing in one spot, of shooting a portrait of a man behind his desk and immediately afterwards a full-face close-up, are quite stupendous. The three lenses, all of which at present have automatic diaphragms, are quite expensive and the single f/2.8 unit which zooms from 36- to 82mm has fairly soft definition at the larger apertures as well as pincushion and barrel distortion. The 85- to 250mm f/4 zoom is far more expensive and the quality of the image it produces is better .

The next few years will see many radical advances in lenses—most for single lens reflexes. It certainly will be interesting to watch if you own a camera.

6

EVERY
PORTRAIT
A DRAMA

People I intend to photograph turn into a petrified forest the moment I unlimber a flood or flash unit and betray the obvious intent to point my reflex in their direction. I don't blame them. I also freeze up in front of a camera. The reaction is universal. If more photographers accepted this as inevitable and recognized the fact that there is no cure, but only prevention, we might be spared the spineless, stuffed, frozen-faced masks which stare out from college and high school yearbooks, the windows of portrait photographers and the albums of too many hobbyists. If your subject freezes, you are beaten before the game begins.

I find that observing people is the best preliminary to shooting a portrait. When I'm with or without a reflex, I watch friends, my family, people I meet, business acquaintances. Mentally, I make notes of their typical expressions, the angles at which they seem best, their habits. When I'm ready to shoot the picture, I will often deliberately maneuver the subject into the chair I wish to use, or position him with the right background and start shooting with no preliminaries. I keep talking to him, watching expressions change and poses alter as he thinks and replies to what I've said. Since I am seldom without a camera, the gentle switch from talking with the camera in my lap to talking with the camera at eye level can be made quickly and naturally. I don't keep the camera up at all times. Instead, I attempt to pre-focus, maintain the same distance and bring the camera to my eye as fast as I can when I see the expression I want. But I continue talking. No matter how excited I may be with the picture possibility, I try to keep perfectly relaxed as if taking a picture were just as relaxing to me as smoking a pipe

Come close with tele: There's one better tactic than keeping your subject at ease by talking to him and that's to have someone else do it. Here, Theodore Mehlin, professor of Astronomy at Williams College discusses the editing of his book with my wife. As Mehlin sat behind his desk, I mounted the 135mm f/3.5 Schneider Tele-Xenar on a Miranda loaded with Plus-X film and backed into a corner of his tiny office where I would be unnoticed. A quick Weston Master meter reading of the palm of my hand held in the same windowlight as the darker side of Mehlin's head indicated a 1/60 at f/5.6 using an exposure index of 200. By moving forward from the corner slightly with the lens set at its closest focusing distance, I cropped my picture area through the viewfinder as precisely as possible.

would be to my subject. Quite often I shoot many frames of the subject against a background I have no intention of using, simply to get him relaxed while being photographed. Then, when I really see just what I want to shoot, my most difficult battle with my subject has been won.

I have never been successful in asking a subject to smile. Either I say something to make him smile or I shoot the picture without a smile. Unless the subject has something to smile about he really isn't smiling, so why try for it? This holds true for all expressions. An expression will only be natural when it is truly reflecting the subject's feelings.

Daylight is splendid portrait light

Once you're able to establish rapport with your subject everything else in portraiture falls neatly into place. Lighting? Daylight's the cheapest, easiest to use, the most flattering, the brightest. At night use room light. Don't haul out floods or flash. If you want to be really precise, arrange your home for photography. I know, for instance, just where in the kitchen I can shoot at 1/60 sec., f/2.8 with Plus-X, and just where I can't. I know how the fluorescent lighting fixtures are placed and just what effect I can expect from them at any given spot in the kitchen. This also holds true for my living room. When I'm visiting, I try to appraise the room and its possibilities beforehand. If there's a portrait I want, I may or may not be able to haul out an exposure meter to check exposure. The presence of a meter may frighten the subject. I've learned to guess exposure indoors. Here's how. When I have a chance, and people aren't around, I try to estimate exposure. Then I check my guess with a meter. By sticking to just a few films, Plus-X and Tri-X and High Speed Ektachrome, I can now generally hit the exposure on the head, set the camera while talking, raise it to my eye while discussing politics and finish a roll of 36 pictures before the subject's really aware I've taken three. If you shoot the same people more than once (I do) they will gradually relax and you'll be able to accomplish more by directing and change of

How to get variety: Never let a portrait possibility go with just one situation or just one shot such as the picture on page 76. Here you see what I term the classical and safe way of making sure you get at least one good portrait and maybe more. I began shooting in Professor Mehlin's office, varying camera distance from head and shoulder to just head. When the phone rang I used it as a natural prop, although the shots with it didn't turn out as well as others. While shooting the professor's face, I noticed his hands on the desk and switched from one frame to these. (An expressive pair of hands alone, I feel, can make a fine portrait.) After the pictures made in his office with my wife keeping him in conversation, Professor Mehlin was more relaxed in the presence of the camera. Thus, when I went back to his house, I had no trouble in approaching him with a 58mm Biotar lens for a portrait as he stood, pipe in hand, in the doorway between rooms. I might have continued shooting with the 135mm Tele-Xenar which I had used in his office, but the long focal length made it impossible for me to get far enough away from the subject indoors to achieve what I wanted—a ¾ view as Professor Mehlin leaned against the door. The exposure here was 1/60 sec. at f/5.6 using Plus-X film again.

Two other approaches: Here are two further enlargements from the good shots picked from the contact sheet on page 78. Frankly, I was quite pleased at the sharpness of Professor Mehlin's hands. The windowlight caught the texture just right and the depth of field of the 135mm Schneider Tele-Xenar when stopped down to f/5.6 can be seen graphically by examining the typed sheet under the hands. The hands, the watch and most of the pencil are sufficiently within the depth of field to produce an impression of extreme sharpness. I doubt if I could have achieved better results with a studio lighting setup if I had labored all day. Certainly it wouldn't have looked as natural, because this shot *is* natural and unposed. The portrait at right can only be achieved when you really have established complete rapport with the subject and you can get him to relax completely. It would be easy to give you countless reasons why I placed the subject just so against the background and why I threw it just so far out of focus and no more. Actually, it simply was a result of the angle at which I approached the subject and the aperture (f/5.6) that was used on the 58mm Biotar lens. If I paid much attention to the background, it was purely unconscious. I think that most backgrounds which photographers claim were the result of much artistic thought are the product of just such deep concentration as I gave this. I admit, however, that I did avoid getting the subject directly in front of the black vertical open doorway, because that would have spoiled the picture.

position—"light that pipe again, turn your head a bit more toward me, lean forward"—all while talking of other things, of course. That is the secret.

For dramatic highlight and shadow pictures where you are more interested in conveying a mood than in showing a face, direct sunlight streaming in a window will do it nicely for you, as witness portrait of the pipe smoker, page 76.

Men, of course, can stand a stronger cross-lighting than women. Ladies may allow certain facial lines to appear, but they'll object to showing every pore or dab of powder, and I don't blame them.

Indoors at night when there's no daylight available, I much prefer overhead lighting fixtures to lamps for portraiture. Overhead fluorescents are my favorite light source for black-and-white and also with color when the proper filters are used (see pages 46 and 47). Lamplight, like daylight, I find too directional. One side of a face is bound to be in shadow, while the other side catches the direct lamplight. This works out well for dramatic photos, but is not too good for most portraits. Of course, you can have your subject turn his or her head directly into the lamplight and shoot across, underneath the lamp. But this is a faked setup and, I feel, will look it.

Outdoors, I feel the light from a dull to bright overcast day is preferable for portraits both from a posing and from a photographic quality point

Avoid these errors: If you're stuck with a 45 to 58mm lens but still want to take closeup portraits here are three pitfalls to avoid. At far left a hand held too far in front of the subject and too close to the camera seems overly large. In the center, what is actually a small nose takes on larger proportions and the head seems elongated at an 18 to 24 in. distance. At right you can see the danger of shooting from above with the lens too close to the forehead. The face becomes a triangle with a pointy chin. If you shoot upwards, the reverse is true. The cure? Get further back or change to a longer lens.

of view. Direct sunlight is very harsh. I find bright shade on a sunlit day nice for color, but too bland for black and white, except for portraits of girls where the softness of the light yields excellent skin texture. Direct bright overcast light, however, yields the most detail. I think that detail in faces, both men's and women's, is vital in creating a good representation of their personality. Facial lines are important. A grand lady at 50 looking a regal 50 is far better to me than a 50-year-old woman trying to look a kittenish 32. It's my own personal opinion, and I'll stick by it.

Two major sins I've noticed in reflex camera handling in portraits are: 1. Approaching too close to the subject. 2. Not getting close enough. Oddly enough, your best camera distance depends greatly upon the focal length of the lens you're using. If you have a noninterchangeable lens reflex and are stuck with a 45 to 50mm focal length, stick to full waist-to-head portraits. Don't come closer, or the results of apparent distortion will become quite evident. (See pictures directly above). If you have a camera allowing you to interchange lenses, purchase a 100 to 135mm lens and really close in on your subject. Not having a long lens today with a single-lens reflex is something akin to a crime. Elsewhere in this book I've suggested sufficient short cuts—in bulk film loading or not investing in floods—to allow you the luxury of spending a $24 or so on a 135mm f/3.5 preset lens. While these

Try odd horizontal compositions: Portraits can also be grab shots such as this one of noted microbiologist Roman Vishniac. He and a group of friends had just returned from a walk in the woods to search for and identify mushrooms. I had loaded my Miranda with Plux-X film in the expectation of shooting some mushroom closeups using a 58mm f/2 Biotar. Dr. Vishniac, watching an automobile being loaded with our gear, leaned against a tree. I estimated exposure for late afternoon at f/11 at 1/60 and shot one negative only, because the subject moved.

inexpensive lenses at full aperture may not be the equal of the better Nikkors or Rokkors or Soligors or Takumars or Schneiders or Steinheils, they are fairly crisp at f/5.6 or so. You'll have to close down to just about that point anyway to get sufficient depth in your portrait to produce an acceptable amount of subject sharpness.

Fill your prism finder

No matter what lens you use, learn to come close enough to your subject so that there isn't an inch of spare picture area in your viewfinder. The better you frame the portrait initially, the less enlargement it will need from the negative and the final print will be sharper.

Don't skimp on film. You're saving plenty if you're shooting bulk film. (If you're using color try not to think of the expense all the time.) See that each shot is varied. Change angles slightly, let the subject change position, change camera-to-subject distance. A roll of 36 pictures is not too much for a single portrait. Here's a good portrait procedure which offers you many

Was the right lens used?: Would this portrait have been better if shot with a longer lens than the 55mm Steinheil used? While I like both pictures made seconds apart as Dr. Vishniac leaned across the card table, there are small points which bother me. The hands seem too large for the face. The background is distracting, particularly the plants. A longer lens would have eliminated both, but in this grab shot on Panatomic-X film I had no time to change lenses or pay enough attention to the background.

variations and the possibility of getting more than one good portrait: Start out at full figure distance using a 50mm or wide angle lens. Shoot your subject in connection with his or her environmental background. Change to a 100- or 135mm and close in for a head and shoulder shot using the subjects hands as part of the portrait. Finally, focus your lens just about as close as it can go and really move in for a full face shot. On a 36-exposure roll, such a procedure would give you 12 shots at each distance. If you vary angle, facial expression and hand position with each shot, you'll have a splendid number of chances for the perfect portrait.

As far as exposure is concerned, expose fully for the darkest area in which you want to hold detail. Try to keep your shutter speed up to $\frac{1}{50}$ or $\frac{1}{60}$ sec. Oh, it's possible to shoot all your portraits at $\frac{1}{30}$ sec., but they won't be as sharp as at $\frac{1}{60}$ even if you're as steady as Gibraltar. Steadiness is quite relative. Next time a photographer proudly asserts that he can hand-hold all his shots at $\frac{1}{30}$ to $\frac{1}{15}$ or slower, look at his shots and see how sharp they are. I know of only a handful of photographers capable of this trick. Practice will help you sharpen your long exposures.

Sharpness is important. In a portrait there is only one place to focus—on the eyes. When you talk to someone you look at their eyes and so this is the most essential part of a portrait. Eyes must be sharp. Ears can be out of focus and noses unsharp. If the eyes are not on a plane with the camera, focus on the near eye.

Here are a few other things to keep in mind when shooting portraits: Keep hands, shoulders, feet quite close to the body, especially when using a normal lens at a fairly close distance. If you don't, they'll seem overly large in your final print. Don't shoot bald men from above, you'll have too much bare skin at eye level. When photographing round faced people try directional light to highlight half the face, leaving the other half partially in shadow. It will cut down the apparent width of the face. If this isn't possible avoid full face portraits of full faced people. When dealing with large noses, find the angle where the nose seems least prominent. Hook noses look best when the owner looks directly into the camera lens. Shoot from an angle where the end of the nose doesn't give the appearance of hooking downwards. Don't attempt to apply makeup to a bad complexion. Only an expert artist can be successful, and often he isn't either. Rely on soft lighting not to pick up blemishes. Don't let your subject overcomb his or her hair. Hair is composed of individual strands and should not look glued together. Avoid splotchy light such as direct sunlight filtering through tree branches unless you like splotchy people. Make the most of props such as cigarettes and pipes. When you see a person in a perfect position for a portrait, don't waste time, get your camera and shoot.

Two more portraits: Is the picture at left, made on Plus-X with a Miranda and 55mm f/1.9 Steinheil Auto-Quinon lens, a portrait or not? The subject was unaware I had made it until she saw the print. Most people turn the picture on its side to see the girl. Below you see one of the first portraits I made with the single-lens reflex. My mother was looking out her living room window on a dull overcast day. The Exakta VX with 58mm Biotar lens was loaded with Super-XX (now discontinued). I shot a whole film roll. I don't think the portrait would be as good if the face had no texture.

$$\boxed{7}$$

PUTTING
SNAP
INTO
SCENICS

"Avoid shooting picture postcard scenics" is the well-intentioned advice many professional photographers give to amateurs. It's quite easy for the professional to avoid them too. He embarks for distant shores solely to shoot pictures. He takes his time, checks the lighting, comes back when it's just right. He travels to exotic parts of the world at other's expense, shows a press card, gets public relations officers to roll out red carpets, and concentrates on nothing but his photography.

To even the most avid amateur or semi-professional photographer travelling on his own, such photography is sheer daydream. Most of us take pictures on vacations and trips when our families, our husbands or wives slow up slightly between shopping, eating and sight-seeing. The very constabulary which might divert cars and buses to aid the professional finds our tripod or camera position blocking traffic and shoos us away.

I fall between the two extremes simply because my wife, while an avid sight-seer and shopper, is a good amateur photographer and thus has more compassion than most families do for my photographic foibles.

You must make time

You must convince your traveling companions that photography is just as important and serious to you as their purchasing, museum going, sightseeing, gastronomical enjoyments are to them. If you allow them their

Fit the lens to the scene: This Venetian gondola prow was photographed with a 135mm f/2.8 Tele-Iscaron lens on a Miranda. On a European vacation, my wife and I searched Venice for a gondola with flowers in a small holder at the prow. (All gondolas had holders but few kept them filled.) In late afternoon, we found one. The gondola rolled with each stroke of the paddle while I tried various focal length lenses. The 135mm framed the flowers properly while maintaining the majesty of the gondola prow. Both 35mm and 58mm lenses made the prow appear too small. I shot the same flowers over 20 times in both black and white and color, using various backgrounds. Exposure was 1/60 sec. at f/5.6. The prism finder indicated precisely how far the bow and the bridges were out of focus. Some people like the color shot with the red and yellow roses best. Others prefer this black and white.

Noon is bad except . . . : During the noon hours I generally put my camera away and go to sleep. Overhead sunlight's bad for almost all scenics. I was trying some closeups of flowers in a field, however, when I looked at one of my favorite trees which I had often meant to photograph. It was being used by a herd of cows for their own siesta. I had only a 50mm f/1.9 Schneider Xenon with me. The Miranda was loaded with Panatomic-X. Using a quick meter reading for the grass, I shot at 1/125 at f/11, focusing on the tree itself.

pleasures, they must allow you yours. This includes giving you sufficient time to wander by yourself to find the best angle, to change film when necessary, to shoot with relaxation without the prospect of being dragged along protesting as you try to snatch a last picture.

Assuming that you will be successful, I'll devote this chapter to the emancipated photographer who must shoot in the lands where the family doth wander and who must ascribe to some semblance of togetherness with his traveling party. It's just what I have to do and, with some ego, I must admit that I've become quite successful at it.

First, a few simple truths. Despite the nonsense you hear that a good photographer can always find good material in his back yard, it isn't true at all. I have lived a good part of my years in New York City. While I admire

Watch for window shots: Poking my head from the Italian Alpine hotel window, I saw a wagon-load of horses. The driver and friend sat on the veranda enjoying an aperitif. Frantically, I tried various lenses from my fixed position. With the 135mm f/2.8 Tele-Iscaron, I included just the horses and a trace of wagon. The pattern was pleasant, but no more. Suddenly the horses became nervous, started a commotion. The attendants leaped aboard and I had my picture. Miranda, Plus-X, 1/125 sec. at f/8.

its photo stores, museums, theatres and musical events, scenically, it's a slovenly mess unless wrapped in snow, covered by twilight or seen from a distance. There are some exceptions. Buildings such as the U.N., various bridges, plus Rockefeller Center are among the jewels. But they've been shot from just about every angle already.

Why can't I shoot N. Y.?

For years my inability to shoot my home town plagued me and induced a distinct photographic inferiority complex. I carried a camera to and from work, and wherever else I went. While I saw and shot many pictures of people, New York itself didn't materialize on any negatives or transparencies.

So similar, but . . . : Could I get a different shot of St. Peter's in Rome than those available on hundreds of postcards? I found the two students sketching, framed them for a foreground and chose the normal 50mm f/1.9 Schneider Xenon to give me a properly impressive St. Peter's in the background. A longer lens would have produced a bigger cathedral but I would have had far less of it in the picture. I stopped down to f/16 and used my depth of field scale to provide sharpness from foreground to background at 1/125 sec. I waited out many dull moments until the two nuns came along to fill the central void. See results, left, without them.

My sense of security and well being received a welcome boost when *Life Magazine* announced that a well-known photographer's realistic pictures of New York would be printed in a forthcoming issue. They were ghastly. A few years later, a young European photographer, Ernst Haas, did shoot some excellent color impressions of New York. The best were blurred or out-of-focus. Apparently there are only two ways of shooting New York— either as a symphony of overflowing garbage cans and patterns of faceless buildings, or as a blurry colored impressionistic manner much like the visions of a very nearsighted man without his glasses. (My mother, a confirmed New Yorker, seldom wears her glasses on the street because she claims everything looks so much nicer without them. I believe her.)

Visiting New York? Shoot your picture postcards of Times Square, the Statue of Liberty, Grant's Tomb. I won't stop you.

I've always produced my best scenics where the grass grows greener— in someone else's yard. I've found beautiful scenics while visiting friends in the country, vacationing in Canada and in the Caribbean and while travelling in Europe. Find grass, earth and sky, a body of water, buildings of tasteful modernity or antiquity and you have the ingredients for good scenics.

Two basic types of scenics

There are two basic types of scenics. There are those that have sufficient interest to stand on their own. Then there are those which need a helping hand from additional subject material. While you will often get excellent shots with No. 1, more often than not, a bit of No. 2 will improve results.

Using a wide angle: Every 5 minutes in Tobago this net is cast out and pulled in, but we only had one chance at shooting before the natives demanded $5 for posing. (Some generous photographers must have preceded us). In the one net session we did photograph, I shot black and white, my wife shot color. I

First locate the subject. Perhaps it's just a tree whose strange shape interests you (picture, page 90) a beautiful town nestled in a valley (picture, page 97) or an impressive building seen on vacation (picture, page 92). After recognizing the photogenic aspect of the scene, find the best angle at which to photograph it. By walking or riding around the subject and moving back and forth from it, you can examine each of its facets. Watch the view through the prism finder and examine the entire picture area from foreground to background for distracting objects. Also check for trees or other possible framing objects in the foreground. Check whether the landscape looks better if you include as much ground as possible or angled higher to exclude ground and place the subject against the sky. This can all be done very easily through the prism finder.

Once you have two or three possible positions, search for the added interest. People give landscapes dimension and a necessary foreground plane. They can also lead your eye into the scenic (picture, page 97). Traveling companions make excellent scenic props. If you use them, don't let them stare weakly into the camera, thus bouncing the viewer's gaze right back

chose a 35mm f/2.5 Angenieux lens for my Exakta VX to increase the apparent distance of the horizon and also to allow me a fairly close shot while still covering the gathering of the net at its widest point. With a longer lens I would have had to remain back. People might have walked between me and the fishermen.

at him. Ask your people-props to look directly into the landscape, walk into it, examine it, become a part of it.

Undoubtedly you will find several angles and points of view for each scenic and sometimes be completely unable to make up your mind which is best. Don't take chances. Shoot both. If you are uncertain whether the picture makes a good horizontal or a better vertical, don't back off and make a compromise. Shoot one of each. Never back away from a subject. Always try to come as close as possible. Do your cropping in the viewfinder. The more you learn to make your entire picture area work for you, the better will be the quality of your final prints.

Basically, we've been discussing the classic scenic—the building which will conveniently stay put since it has already been there a century or so, the fountain, the valley—all nicely settled subjects perfectly willing to let you scout around for the best angle, the additional bit of interest to enhance the picture. Of course the light may change and shadows lengthen while you ponder the scenic, but that's your problem. Learn to work with reasonable speed.

95

But you have another important variable at your command—choice of lenses. The relatively low cost of interchangeable lenses for reflexes today puts a wide angle 35mm and a 135mm tele or long focus lens within the reach of just about any photographer. The classic traditional lens of scenic photography is the wide angle. I have a good friend who never sets out with more than a wide angle and his normal lens. I wouldn't go anywhere without the 100-, 105- or 135mm lens as well. While it's quite true that the 35mm lens takes in a greater angular sweep, it's equally true that it thereby makes each individual object that much more minute. In addition, the wide angle lens increases apparent distance between foreground and background objects—the valley looks wider, the distant mountains seem further away, the people at the end of the street look more like ants than people. I have seldom found the wide-angle lens a satisfactory instrument for shooting scenics. I resort to it only in one instance—where it is physically impossible for me to include all that I wish in a picture. I much prefer the normal 50- to 58mm lens which does not minimize the dramatic subject material I'm trying to emphasize.

Long lenses for scenics?

Surprisingly, the 100-, 105- or 135mm lens is excellent for scenics. Quite often, viewers of my pictures have insisted the shots must have been made with a wide-angle lens when they were actually the work of a 135mm. If they had been shot with wide angle, the feeling of closeness to the subject, of much activity packed in a small space, of tight composition would have disappeared and become instead a never-ending series of objects getting smaller and smaller as they approached the horizon.

Build planes in depth: Here's the classic landscape that can be dreadfully dull unless it's handled carefully. Climbing to the Brenner Pass from Austria into Italy, you come across the magnificent view of the city of Innsbruck nestled cozily between the foreground heights and the snow capped and clouded peaks in the distance. My wife and I quickly turned off the road, disembarked, unlimbered our cameras and spied two English travellers enjoying lunch and the view. We decided that they would form an excellent foreground and provide dimension to the scenic. They heard us, turned around and asked us to photograph them with their camera. We did, and then requested that they turn back and gaze into the valley, to lead the viewers of our picture into the scene. Our next problem was one of camera height, angle and foreground placement. We elected to position them to the right to balance the large mountains at the left, and then we experimented with several different camera heights. When we stood up and held the camera at eye level, a large railroad yard of no particular beauty appeared in the foreground, and our two Britishers were lost in a maze of detail. (See picture at left.) When we lay prone, the railroad yard disappeared and the two figures were almost silhouetted against the white buildings. We chose a 55mm f/1.9 Steinheil Auto-Quinon lens for the Miranda, which framed the scene just as we wanted it, and made an exposure of 1/125 sec. at f/16 on Plus-X, which gave us complete foreground to background sharpness. The clouds registered perfectly.

Backlight: Fountains and water-falls had always seemed pretty pedestrian photographic fare to me. The water resembles smoky glass stained a tattle tale grey. In Rome, however, while travelling across one of the many piazzas in late afternoon, I saw a shimmering back-lit fountain. What a difference! Just as I unlimbered the Miranda and framed the central portion with the 135mm f/2.8 Tele-Iscaron lens, a breeze sprang up angling the return spray away from the central horse figure. Would the breeze die before the sun left? It did, and an exposure of f/11 at 1/250 sec. on Plus-X stopped the spray sufficiently. Afterwards I walked around to the opposite side of the fount and made another exposure (left) to show how important backlight really is.

When shooting a classic scenic, I seldom start with the wide angle lens or the normal. I first try the 135mm. Naturally, it will limit the angle of view. Since your eyes are taking in nearly 180 degrees and are being very impressed with what they see, the far narrower angle of the 135mm may at first seem like a travesty on the scene. But since we can't project that glorious scenic in panoramic three dimensions and in color, as we really see it, let's discover if we can achieve something equally valid and dramatic.

Before you put the 135mm down and reach for the wide angle, examine the view carefully through the prism finder as you would a distant scene through a telescope. Since you're actually looking through the lens of the camera, you'll see the apparent perspective changes. Note how distant buildings seem less far in relation to the foreground. Move your 135mm lens slowly and carefully over the scene, attempting to isolate interesting parts of the overall view. If you do find a good interesting composition but can't get it all in the finder, instead of changing lenses, try moving back until you are able to get the very minimum squeezed into the picture area. After a few shots with the 135-, 105- or 100mm lens, try the 35mm or 50mm lens if you wish, and restudy the scene. You may find the scenic much less exciting through the prism finder.

I've often shot scenes with wide angle lenses and later remarked, on seeing the picture, "Well, it's not too interesting, but it does give you a good overall shot."

Ergo, for overall views the wideangle lens is often the best choice. For the more dramatic photograph, check the view first through a longer focal length.

Focus is an extremely important tool in landscapes. Generally I find that the landscapes rendered sharp from foreground to background are more interesting than those in which some planes are sharp and some not. This may seem slightly contrary to the visual conception presented herein, since we did open this chapter with a scenic violating this rule. But the gondola prow on page 88 is purely an impressionistic view. The majority of scenics— and the majority which appear in this book—are sharp.

Cameras whose diaphragms reopen to full aperture when the film is wound to the next exposure can be used for visual checks by setting the aperture and viewing the picture before winding the film. Other cameras have special depth of field preview buttons. With leaf-shutter reflexes, there's no way to check depth of field.

Put the depth of field scale to work

But be not disheartened. For really first class scenics, you can't rely purely on a visual check. An object which may seem sharp in the prism finder may not be as clearly defined as you thought when the negative is enlarged or the transparency projected on a good sized screen. To insure sharpness, use the depth of field scale on the lens mount. Don't focus on the principal object in the scene and then shoot—get the most depth of field for your exposure. Focus on the nearest and the furthest objects which you wish to include in your picture and read the distances on the footage scale. These two distance settings must fall between the aperture settings on the depth of field scale. If they don't, select a smaller aperture which can encompass them. This is precisely how the picture on page 92 was made. One of the hardest bad habits to cure is quickly focusing on the central point of interest and shooting. Let your depth of field scale work for you. I'm always shocked to see how few people take advantage of it when shooting scenics.

By now it should be apparent that building and shooting a good scenic is a precise photographic task which cannot be trusted to luck. A static scene can be recorded properly only if you keep in mind a host of variables— angle, distance, foreground objects, lighting, choice of lens. Perhaps you're feeling that sufficient attention to all these items will probably prevent you from ever getting a picture shot at all. You may be right—in your first few tries anyway. Shooting a scenic is much like learning to drive a car. At first it seems impossible to sort out all the pedals, watch the speedometer, steer and pay attention to fellow travelers on the road. Too much seems to be happening at once. Yet, look around you at the large numbers of skilled automobile drivers. And bus drivers seems to be able to make change, open and shut doors, and give directions in addition.

As in driving, shooting the perfect scenic with due care for all the amenities takes practice before it becomes second nature to you. Run through all the possibilities a number of times with each subject and the procedure will begin to click into place as in a computing machine. It's true that good scenics can sometimes be the result of pure luck. But consistently good scenics aren't.

At first, to cover yourself so you don't wind up with no picture at all, take that first impression of the scenic as you see it. Then, having committed it to film, you may feel more relaxed while trying to refine your concept of the scene.

The way in which you go about refining it—the particular tricks you develop in framing, focusing and finding different angles—will in time form the basis of your photographic style. When a viewer starts to pick your scenics from others purely on the basis of individual approach, you've progressed quite satisfactorily.

So much for the classic approach to the scenic. We now reach the grab shot stage of scenics where you come upon or have given to you the perfect or almost perfect scenic which must be shot on a now-or-never basis. Two men load horses on a cart (picture, page 91) fishermen pull in a net (picture, pages 94 and 95). You must be ready.

It seems almost banal to insist that you keep your camera loaded and out of the case. Just how to accomplish this is explained in "Chapter 12." In any event, an empty camera lying dormant in an everready case or gadget bag might just as well have stayed home and never have traveled at all.

If you're a professional photographer, you can always be ready by using

Lending the planes a hand: A young mother in a housecoat hangs out an early morning wash under the watchful eye of Super-XX film, a 58mm f/2 Biotar lens and an Exakta VX set to f/16 at 1/250 sec. For this scenic the separation of planes is essential in the overall impression of the picture. While there was a definate fog rolling in the distant valley, I confess that a bit of dodging during enlarging brought it out more precisely and the clouds did need some burning in. Using a comparatively grainy high speed film outdoors such as the long ago discontinued Super-XX is a folly I have since outgrown.

three cameras, one with a wide angle, one with a normal and one with a tele lens. You swing the first over your right shoulder, carry a second on the left shoulder, and let the third hang around your neck. Thus decked out like a photographic Christmas tree, you sally forth to take charge of whatever may happen—provided of course, you grab the right camera at the right time and don't get all the neck straps tangled.

Most of us can simplify matters considerably. We don't have more than one or possibly two cameras. My favorite scenic grab shot lens, held at the ready, is the normal 50- to 58mm. The 58mm lens is a perfect compromise for one lens. But if you gave me my choice of two focal lengths, I'd pick a tele and wide angle.

Shoot first and then . . .

How can you handle the instant scenic? Shoot first and ask questions later.

The variations of the instant scenic are many—shots through a train window, through a car windshield, out the window of your home or hotel. Unless you are actually on the move in a train, plane or car, a careful analysis of the instant scenic will reveal that it's not completely instant. What is instant, however, is the event taking place within the picture area which makes it imperative that you take the picture when you see it and not waste time.

Presetting your exposure helps. I always try to keep my camera properly set for the prevailing light conditions so I don't have to start calculating exposure if I see a good instant scenic. I know many people who also preset distances depending on the depth of field to pull them through. It seldom pulls me through. I would rely instead on a faster shutter speed, $\frac{1}{125}$ sec. or better, with an attending larger aperture and possible loss in overall sharpness. There's method in this. If this is an instant scenic capable of changing swiftly at any given time, there's a good possibility that I'm actually shooting some sort of action. I'd rather risk a slightly out-of-focus foreground or background than blur the moving central subject material. This is just a matter of personal decision, and you may come up with just the opposite technique yourself.

Should you prefocus?

I have never been happy presetting the focus. Instead, I've learned to focus in almost the same short instant it takes to press the shutter release. If I'm slightly off, the depth of field will probably cover my error. Where do I focus? Not necessarily on the main subject. If the main subject is close to the foreground, I try to focus slightly behind it. If it's distant, I move the focus in front of it. Of course what I'm trying to do in a rather primitive way is to gain the maximum depth of field without resorting to my depth of field tables, depth of field scale, or preview button. When shooting fast, a preview button is undeniably a great help.

In grab scenics, shoot immediately. Then move in and try to improve your composition by cutting out non-working picture area. Vary angle, find

One bridge, two shots: Seldom am I so certain of my ability that I walk away after one shot convinced I have the picture. Generally I change angles, lenses, distances, to cover all possibilities. In Florence I photographed the Ponte Vecchio over the Arno with the sun behind it. The water was relatively still, the picture framed just so, with the 135mm f/2.8 Tele-Iscaron on the Miranda. The human figures seem perfect. I made two different shots and turned away in blissful euphoria, convinced I had precisely what I wanted. The second picture is on the next page. Exposure? Don't remember, but the film was Plus-X.

a better view, change lenses if you have time. If it's a truly instant scenic, you will get one picture only. But always try for the better one.

Occasionally you will be smitten with one scene, one angle, one composition, one perspective. You find a scenic, maneuver to the right angle, choose a lens and shoot. You will feel that the picture is perfect. If you're pig-headed, like the author, you will discontinue any attempt at improving the situation. I advise against this, although the one time that it has happened to me I did in fact shoot two quite good scenics (pictures, above and next page).

Hints, tips and advices concerning scenics can stretch from here to infinity, but rather than bore you with endless verbiage, I've gathered some of the yet undiscussed problems for the end of this chapter, and will deal with them concisely. You may agree with some, disagree with others. They represent merely the sum of my own experience and should be used only as guideposts, no matter how emphatically I may insist that only an idiot would do other than I say.

Color vs. black and white: After listening to many a lecture on how color must be handled quite differently from black and white, I've come to

the conclusion that they should be used on exactly the same subjects in the same manner. I've seldom seen a black-and-white picture that didn't look equally stunning in color and vice-versa. Oh yes, I can think of one exception. I've photographed a number of color sunsets in which delicate changes in color actually were the sole ingredients of the picture. Naturally, such subject material is better in color than in black and white. I would say that black-and-white scenics are harder to handle than color. In black and white you must depend on changes in mass, in contour and line, in focus, to delineate one subject from another within the picture area. In color, color itself will often pinpoint an object which, in black and white, would blend right into the background. This ability to make a good photographer look great and save a poor one from throwing his camera away after the first roll of scenics, accounts, in part, for the popularity of color film. An incisive, highly imaginative photographic brain may be needed to create a good scenic photograph from a subject in black and white. The same subject in color may look wonderful with no more than beginner's luck.

Concentrate on difference of black and white

In any event, don't attempt to analyze how a subject must be handled differently for color. Work the other way around. Try to discover how to maintain interest in black and white if the subject is robbed of all its color.

Lighting: Although I've often insisted that photographers must go back and re-examine a subject at various times of the day under several lighting situations, I've rarely had time to do it myself. But scenics do look most interesting if cross-lit, with the sun at right or left, or back-lit with the sun shining towards the camera from a sky position out of lens range. The reasoning is quite simple. Cross and back light separate the various planes within the scenic and give each some shadow detail which serves to separate subjects within each plane. I try to avoid shooting around noon, when there are no shadows and everything blends into everything else. Front light seems to make most scenics appear as cardboard cutouts with shadows behind each object.

Fountains and waterfalls look most dramatic when backlit to enhance the sparkle of the water. Buildings look best when crosslit so shadows can delineate the detail and sculpture on the façades. Overcast, while a splendid light for photographing people, just does absolutely nothing for scenics.

Filters: In my early photographic days, I remember paying what to me was a small fortune for a set of red, green and yellow filters made in Switzerland. They came in a plush-lined, fitted-leather case, and I adored looking at them. That's the most enjoyment I ever received from any filters for black-and-white photography. Today's black-and-white films record sky, clouds, and foliage very nicely indeed (see picture, page 97) and I've found even a yellow filter unnecessary for shooting scenics. I will admit that a craving for a violently dramatic black sky and billowy white clouds can only be satisfied with a red filter. After a few such dramatic sorties, your red filter will wind up next to mine.

In color, there is far more reason for using color correction and compensation filters. Most films, when used for distant scenics may record them with a bluish cast. If you find this occurring in your scenics, try a Skylight filter which will "warm" the picture slightly and remove the bluish coloration. You may, however, find you only need it with particular lenses. Some lenses produce transparencies which are warmer and more yellow. Others produce pictures which are colder and slightly bluish. Try your lenses before committing yourself. I must admit that I either like slightly colder pictures, can't tell the difference, or have a set of warm lenses. I've never used a Skylight filter.

8

DO
STRANGERS
BITE?

Most pictures that you'll take with your eye-level reflex will require precise technique and intelligent composition. But photographing people you don't know will also require nerve.

Many photographers never outlive their fear of the unknown person at the other end of the lens. I have a friend, an excellent photographer of buildings, of patterns, of scenics who has yet to go beyond photographing a stranger's back. Although he tells himself he just doesn't care to take pictures of people, the truth lies closer to utter panic.

Actually, he is missing a most satisfying, interesting, thought-provoking, friendship-making area of photography. I don't consider myself an aggressive photographer, but I have learned the photographs that can be made of people are worth the difficulties inherent in overcoming my own timidity.

Unhappily, few photographic writers and teachers have had sufficient experience with such subject material to pass on any concrete advice. Some photographic teachers merely suggest you hide the camera, shoot quickly then run.

I don't believe in running from any subject—friend or stranger. Such behavior indicates that you feel you are engaged in some illegal or immoral action—a deed of which you are ashamed. A smile on your face and the camera in plain view will generally produce more cordial relations, even in regions where a stranger with camera is looked upon as a scourge.

Never photograph a person in a position or action you yourself would find embarrassing, annoying or antagonizing. Never invade another human being's right of privacy, no matter how tempting it may seem. Too many photographers attempt to record people making love, washing clothes in the river, padding about barefoot, wearing dirty and torn clothes. Such docu-

Politeness plus a tele: Any woman tourist wearing slacks or immodest dress who attempts to enter St. Mark's Cathedral in Venice will be stopped by this impressive gentleman. He will raise his baton, barring the way from the outer vestibule into the main building. With all the people between us entering and leaving, it was barely possible to get a clear shot with the 135mm f/2.8 Tele-Iscaron on my Miranda. I persisted, and finally made three negatives at f/4 at 1/30 sec. on Plus-X. He then became quite perturbed about being photographed, and motioned me to desist taking pictures. I waved as graciously as possible in his direction and left. If I had hesitated I might never have gotten a picture.

mentation is considered high art in some circles. If you see people washing their clothes in water running in the gutter, as I did in Tobago, British West Indies, you will make untold scores of friends and undo much damage caused by other unthinking photographers by *not* taking the picture.

It's up to you to convince strangers in English, in sign language, by Berlitz phrase book, or in any other way you know, that you want to take honest and truthful pictures home. The minute they receive the slightest indication that you presume to be the rich, English-speaking, superior, camera-toting tourist who wants to record only poverty and embarrassing moments, pack up your camera and go home. You're finished.

People's attitudes concerning photographers vary from country to country. In my experience, for instance, I have found that Italians—all Italians—enjoy being photographed. The mountain villagers between Rome and Florence will consider it an honor if you stop your car.

In the Caribbean area, much overrun by tourists, you will find the opposite attitude—resentment, suspicion, anger. The outstretched hand often demands compensation for pictures. I noted, however, that even the surliest native found it difficult to be anti-tourist if you show a genuine interest in their villages and the children.

No one will see what you don't shoot

One of the really knowledgeable photographers that I know, Alfred Eisenstaedt, one day revealed why he is trusted and liked by just about every notable figure he has ever photographed. "If I see a person I wish to photograph in a pose or action I feel he wouldn't like reproduced, I warn him," explains Eisie. "Suppose I want to photograph a politician but I see a liquor glass in his hand or on a table nearby, I suggest that it would be best if the glass did not appear. Usually he is very grateful that I've looked out after his interests. Even a professional photographer has a great deal of control over what pictures of his are published. When I see a picture I don't want published, I don't shoot it. No editor can publish what I don't shoot."

Now to the actual techniques of shooting strangers with a reflex. First, avoid resembling a traveling camera store (see "Chapter 12" on how and what to carry). Carry only one camera from your gadget bag at a time. Don't keep it in an everready case. Hang it from a neckstrap locked to the

Don't dawdle: This barbershop in Tobago had me stumped. The variation in light level between inside and outside was tremendous. If I used my meter and pointed it at the barbershop all eyes would have turned on me. I moved away and, in the shade, took a substitute reading from the palm of my hand. I used one lens opening larger than the meter indicated because of the variation in tone between my subjects and my palm. With the Exakta VX set at f/11 and 1/50 sec., I shot quickly using a 135mm f/4 Zeiss Triotar. The film was Panatomic-X. I immediately moved away again, placed the Triotar on my other Exakta body loaded with Anscochrome, and reshot. If you can imagine this scene in delicate pastels, you can see why I wanted the color too.

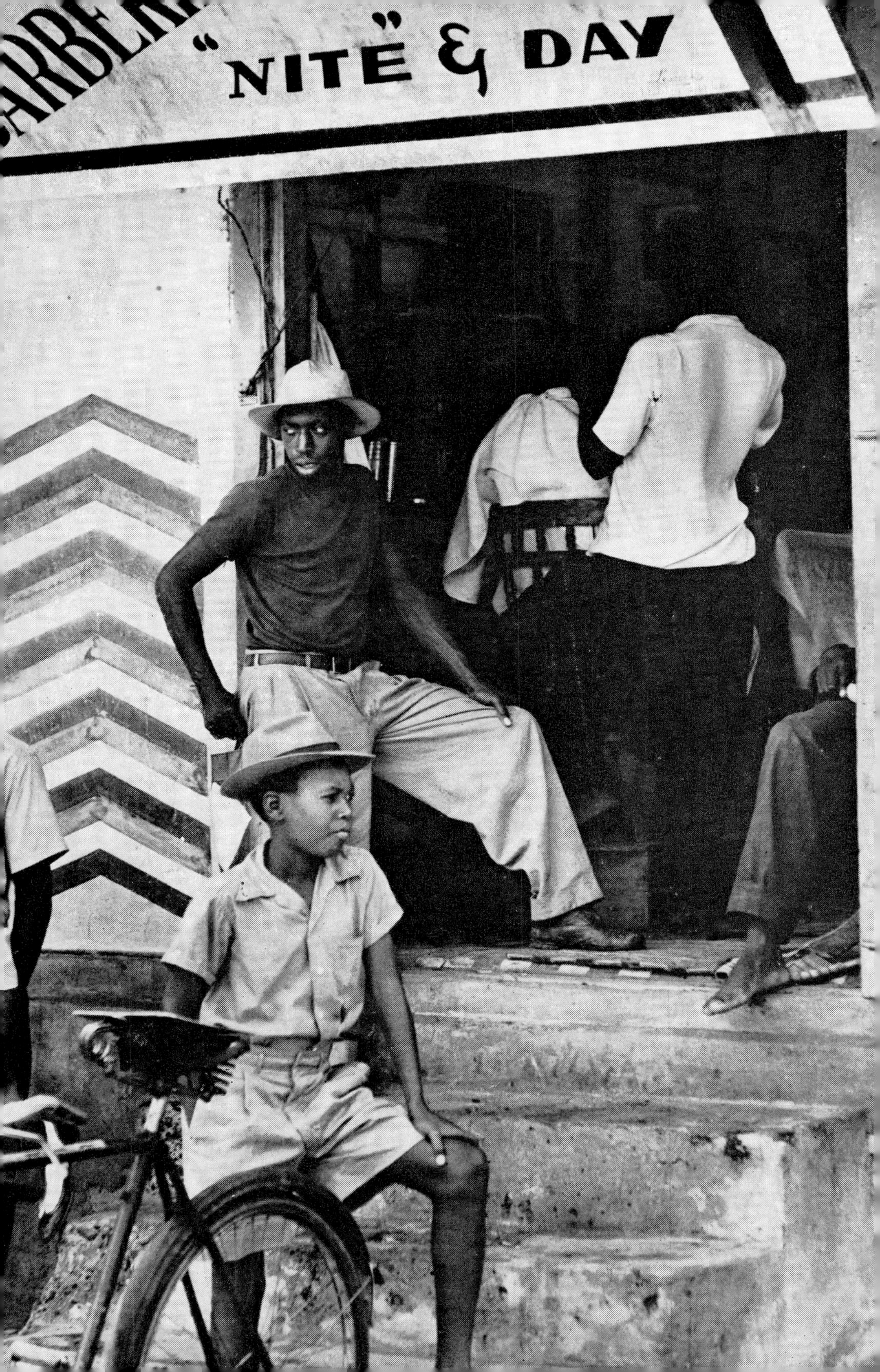
"NITE" & DAY

Some are unfriendly: The expressions on the Tobagonian children above immediately reveal a less than friendly attitude towards the photographer. We came
upon them far from town on a remote point from whence we were hiring a boat
and guide to take us skin diving. Only the fact that we were negotiating with
their elders for the boat-hire stopped them from preventing my photography.
In the boat, I had been using a 58mm Biotar f/2 on the Exakta, and dared not
attempt to change to a more suitable 135mm lens. Hence, the enlarged and
distorted front elbow. Later, after many visits to the point, and longer acquaint-
ance, the boys grew friendly and relaxed. Making friends from unwilling subjects
provides me with a very challenging but rewarding task. The shot here was made
at about f/16, 1/50 sec. on Panatomic-X film. Dark eye shadows were caused by
noon sunlight.

But others are friendly: These two groups represent the absolute extremes in
my pictures of strangers. At left is a group of women in the Italian mountain town
of Barberino val d'Elsa, sitting in a doorway, hard at work embroidering. Our
tiny car sped past this town before I knew it, and after going several miles, my
wife and I decided we should return. The village was ancient and pock-marked
from World War II machine gun bullets. Only women and a few old men were in
evidence. Every woman was embroidering and almost every worker wore glasses
at the tip of her nose. The villagers were courteous, and proud that we had
selected to photograph them. We wandered through the village, and had difficulty
preventing the villagers from lining up in a row to pose for us. I tried to catch
this group unaware with my Miranda and 135mm Tele-Iscaron lens, but didn't
quite make it. Still, perhaps their friendly faces turned in our direction is the
better picture anyway. Exposure on Plus-X film was about f/11 at 1/125 sec.

113

two eyelets. Secure a sunshade to the front of the lens. You will most likely be advised by many photographers not to carry your reflex over your shoulder. They insist it should be carried around your neck. I disagree with this arrangement. Carrying a camera on your chest with the lens pointed away from you at any and all subjects is in bad taste. It disturbs people much like chewing food with your mouth open.

I do agree that a shoulder is not the place to sling a camera. It takes far too long to unlimber the camera and get it ready to shoot. There's always a good chance that the strap may slip from your shoulder. (A friend, Bob Schwalberg, began sewing buttons on the shoulders of his coats to prevent this very thing, but that's going to extremes for most of us.) I wrap the neckstrap securely around my right wrist, (I'm right handed) grab the camera in my hand and walk along as if I were carrying a parcel.

Now for details. Try Plus-X film outdoors, Tri-X indoors. For most photographs keep your shutter speed up to ⅛₂₅ sec. if you can, but don't go lower than ⅛₀ or ⅕₀ sec. Take an overall reading of objects close at hand in the same lighting as your subject, and set your camera accordingly.

In the lens department, I'd recommend a 135mm. It allows you to remain a respectable distance from your subject. I've found many strangers don't really object to being photographed so much as they dislike the indignity of a lens thrust close to their faces.

When the subject has a definite connection with his or her background, plan on using as small a lens opening as possible. Try a wide aperture if the background detracts from the subject. Unlike regular portraiture where I often prefer no background, I've generally found the backgrounds behind strangers extremely important.

I always try to keep on the move until I'm sure of what I want to shoot and how I will shoot it. Then I stop, place my feet two feet or more apart for firm, steady support, take half a breath, and, using the neckstrap around my wrist for support like a rifle sling, shoot the picture. The movement from camera at side to camera at eye level should be almost instantaneous. Once you have taken one picture, don't pretend that you never took a picture at all, by hiding the camera behind your back. Keep the camera in view. Even if the subject looks apprehensive, try for a second and better shot, perhaps moving in slightly to crop the picture further.

Don't think that walking up to a possible subject and requesting permission to take a picture always solves the problem. You may get coopera-

Still a tele helped: The majesty and grace of the Barberino val d'Elsa women was mainly responsible for our stop to photograph them. Of all the women my wife and I encountered, this lady was the most interesting and dignified. We felt that she must have been a great beauty when young, and we attempted to convey this feeling. Since I wished to delineate facial texture and prevent shadow detail from disappearing, I gave this picture one lens opening more exposure than I had indicated by a meter reading from the palm of my hand in the sunlight. Exposure on Plus-X was f/5.6 at 1/60 sec. using the 135mm f/2.8 Tele-Iscaron lens on the Miranda. A 135mm lens or thereabouts is almost an essential in keeping a distance from your subject. Get too close and even the friendliest will become restless.

Fellow sightseers: It was almost impossible to shoot any decent pictures during the group sightseeing tour through Rome. We were always on the move, and you can't keep 31 bus passengers waiting long. Rather than give up entirely, I concentrated efforts on my fascinating fellow sightseers. Everyone gathered around the guide while he explained the Roman forum below. I was delighted with the lady at left, and made one picture with the 55mm f/1.9 Steinheil Auto-Quinon on the Miranda. Exposure was about f/11 at 1/60 sec. using Plus-X film. Both guide and tourists were too engrossed to notice me.

Indifferent but photographable: The overpoweringly muscled gentleman at right is Anthony, naturalist, guide and skin diver of Tobago in the Carribean. At first I thought of asking him to remove the mask and snorkel, but I then became fascinated by the white pipe against the rich, dark skin. Anthony was proud of his physique and, while not acknowledging that I was taking his picture, he obligingly struck poses that were a delight. Since the scene was heavily backlit, I took a Weston Master III reading close to Anthony for skin tone. Exposure with the 55mm f/1.9 Steinheil Auto-Quinon, Miranda camera, and Panatomic-X was about f/4 at 1/60.

116

tion—too much of it. The subject combs his hair, puts his best foot forward and smiles.

On the whole, I've found most U.S. and British citizens quite agreeable to being photographed as long as they feel they are being portrayed in a dignified manner. Americans and Britishers are most tolerant about photography probably because it is so prevalent a hobby in their countries. The few times that I've shot pictures of strangers in New York, my most frequent problem has concerned the people who spy my camera and insist on coming over to discuss photography. Again I must refer to my friend Alfred Eisenstaedt, who has devised a way out of this predicament. When people come over to talk to him he keeps right on shooting, explaining as he shoots that he simply must continue shooting to get the pictures he wants, and that he's sure, as people interested in photography, that they understand. Of course, if your main subject comes over for a chat, it's much more of a problem.

If they say "no," ask "why?"

In twenty-odd years of shooting pictures, I've been told many times by subjects that no pictures were to be taken. I have always answered with the same question: "Why?" Quite often the reply you receive will open the way to a friendly discussion in which the "no" can be changed to a "yes." I've found one clinching argument. Offer to send the subject a picture of himself. Few of us can resist a free photograph. When you have your film processed, make sure you *do* send the picture you promised.

In the years that I've been taking pictures of strangers, I've only been stopped once, and I must confess that it was mostly my fault, since I shouldn't have attempted to take the pictures in the first place. I attended a political rally held in Madison Square Garden in New York City for the late Senator Joseph McCarthy. It was obvious to all that I was not cheering and clapping loudly. Instead, I was photographing the people who were. Resenting this, they began to hurl objects in my direction. In essence, they were perfectly justified in resenting being photographed, if not in resorting to violence. I was attempting to portray the personalities of the individuals at the rally. This certainly was not to their best interests.

Stay away from political meetings, rallies or other gatherings where you are not in sympathy with the crowd and they know it.

If the girl's beautiful, should you?: Is it respectable for a married man to photograph beautiful strange girls? Don't think I hadn't pondered this long before I arrived at the affirmative. I was standing on the Ponte Vecchio over the Arno River in Florence, Italy. Unfortunately, the roadway of the bridge was filled with rubble. I thus elected to cut off the lady's feet. Through the prism finder I could see the backlight doing interesting things to the buildings in the rear when I threw them out of focus. Exposure was f/11, 1/60 sec. using a 135mm f/2.8 Tele-Iscaron on a Miranda. Film was Plus-X. A street photographer operated on the bridge also. You can see part of his paraphernalia on the wall at left. Who was this beauty? Whom was she waiting for? Did she speak English?

119

9

PROBLEM
CHILDREN

Children are probably the most satisfying of human photographic subjects. Practically without exception, they delight in being photographed. All are photogenic, even though they may later grow into dire challenges for any camera. Though they are comparatively easy to photograph, they do present a distinct challenge. Photograph them and you will realize why such words as peak action, grab shot, preset exposure, decisive moment, stop-motion shutter speed and hair-trigger response have joined the well-rounded photographer's lexicon. Children don't idle while you analyze your approach. They will not be still. When they are, unhappy faces result. For any sort of success you must often follow the herd like a hunter and shoot them on the run. It's fun but tiring. When you're lucky, a specific activity—swinging, swimming—may keep them located in a specific area.

What types of photographs are we attempting to shoot? Children as they really are—running, playing, enjoying themselves, alone, with adults, and other children. Sunday-clothed, studio-photographed little hellions with their hair slicked in place by adoring mothers are to be avoided. Such pictures may satisfy some mothers, but they don't satisfy me. I find it impossible to believe that a child will appear and act normally in such artificial surroundings.

When I'm with my daughter I always carry a reflex, even though I may not plan to take pictures. Besides conditioning her to the camera, it seems that picture possibilities most often occur when I am not planning to shoot any. Since my camera is present, I can change rapidly from a passive observer to a participant in no more time than it takes to remove a lens cap.

When I'm visiting other children, I always bring a camera and keep it

Swing and shoot: While I photographed friends with a Minolta SR-2 and 100mm f/3.5 Auto-Rokkor lens, this young man, playing soldier, exhibited signs of jealousy. Without turning, I tried to decide whether I should shoot just the one boy or include the two boys behind him. Since there was no background but blank sky, the picture would have lacked cohesiveness with just one. I quickly swung around, framed the head against the chest of the boy behind, eliminated the boy at left and shot at f/11, 1/60 sec. on Plus-X. The second boy's smile adds just enough additional interest, I think. The whole head would have been distracting. This print shows almost the entire negative area.

in view. I explain what it is and how it works if the children are interested, and take practice shots until they become bored watching me and no longer pay any attention.

Use a film no grainier than Kodak Plus-X. While Tri-X can produce splendid results on adult subjects, the greater smoothness of children's skins demands a virtually grainless film. For some reason, viewers examine the skin texture in a child's picture closely and become disturbed when it appears mottled and grainy, as it may when the print is right under his nose. No use in attempting to explain to such people that they're holding the print improperly close. A slow film such as Panatomic-X is perhaps safest.

You can shoot many more closeup shots using the normal focal length prism reflex lens than you can with an adult. Children's noses are small, they seldom adopt poses with their hands closer to the camera than their faces. The risks of a normal lens causing apparent perspective distortion in which close objects appear overly large are less than with grownups. In focusing, if you have a split-image rangefinder, ignore it completely. There are no straight vertical lines in a child's face on which to focus. It's far easier and more accurate to determine sharpness directly on the ground glass focusing screen. As in most photography, the eyes are your best focusing points.

Bend those knees and sit down

Proper shooting height and angle are specially critical when photographing children. Too many photographers limit their pictures to those made from a standing position. Such photographs turn the children into gnomes with large heads and tiny feet—the result of too steep a shooting angle. With few exceptions the child's own level is the proper height at which to take pictures. The camera should be held no higher than the child's eyes. For those of us whose limber days are long past, a waist-level reflex focusing hood in place of the prism finder can be a great help—although it will limit your format to the horizontal.

While a bright overcast day is preferable for adult subjects, it's not essential for children. Deep shadows under their eyes at noon, contrasty sunlight, do not have the same damaging photographic effect. But don't ever expect anyone—even a child—to face into the sun without squinting. The old maxim which advised photographers to take pictures only with the sun over their shoulders should have been layed to rest long ago.

The most essential actions to photograph are those which a child or children participate in naturally. You must be an astute observer. If you're lucky you may be ready, focused, with exposure preset, and catch the action the very first time.

Generally the action—whether skipping rope, playing soldier, jumping in the water, will be over before you've shot half the pictures you want.

At this point many adults make a mistake by reposing the children. Such adult interruption generally incurs a very evident lack of enthusiasm in the subject or subjects. While you can suggest to the children that they repeat the action, if they balk and don't feel enthusiastic forget about it and shoot next time the action takes place. You may have to wait hours or days, but it's worth it. Posed children look either like stiff statues or little

Fill the prism finder: Our fishing guide in Canada, Romeo Lapierre, has 11 lovely childen, all living with him and his wife in a small house that he built near the lake. The first time I asked to photograph them, the Lapierres dressed in their Sunday best, much to my disappointment. A few days later I made a second request. This time the Lapierres felt it too much trouble to dress the children, so I was able to get a more realistic look at them. I noticed the home-made swings in a nearby tree, and asked the children if they would like to play there. They made for the swings like express trains and I had an hour's shooting time with little or no indication that the children realized I was still there. This shot made on Plus-X with a Nikon F, 50mm f/2 Nikkor lens, 1/250 sec., f/11.

Then come closer: Since the two swings were fastened at right angles, the girls had to alternate actions or smash into each other. I switched to the Minolta SR-2 with a 100mm f/3.5 Auto-Rokkor, since I wanted the girls close together yet both fairly large in the picture. The foreshortening effect of the 100mm lens narrowed the apparent distance between the girl in the swing facing me and the one behind. I prefocused on a spot midway between the two girls, checked my depth of field scale and found that I needed an f/16 aperture to get both girls in focus. I cut the shutter speed to 1/125 sec., not fast enough to stop full action, but sufficient if I was lucky enough to catch both girl's at peak of their swing. I was.

Should the mother be cropped out?: This small family group and its offbeat pose has always delighted me. I've never seen anyone else hold a baby quite the way Romeo Lapierre, the Canadian fishing guide does. Jeannette, Romeo's wife, had dressed the baby for picture taking, but the parents had not expected to be included in the photographs, so they were not dressed for the occasion. Actually, I had originally thought of just shooting the father and daughter, but the mother was examining the baby so intently I stepped back a few feet and included her as well. Since her face is not fully shown, she doesn't detract from the father and child but she does serve to lead your eye into the picture. Exposure with Nikon F, 50mm f/2 Nikkor lens was about f/11 at 1/60 sec. on Plus-X film.

Is this too maudlin?: I had been testing a wide angle lens attachment over the regular lens of a Contaflex I camera when I noticed our neighbor's tomboy daughter and her new kitten. The late afternoon sunlight was furnishing a back and cross light which picked up every bit of detail and also produced interesting hair highlights. Without waiting to unscrew the wide angle attachment, I swung the Contaflex around and shot at about f/8, 1/30 sec. on Plus-X. Usually I find such child-animal relationships rather maudlin, but I still like this one. Perhaps because I took it.

hams. That's why child models who can pose naturally do command so much money per hour from professional photographers.

Most artificial light photographs of children are very artificial indeed. Direct light—either flood or flash—produces startled, burnt-out faces with deep shadows and dark backgrounds. If you think that you may shoot a great number of photographs indoors over a considerable period of time, it might be worthwhile to re-plan the illumination of your rooms for photographic as well as purely living purposes. (See pages 79 to 82.) In addition, light from a flash or flood, when bounced from the ceiling, will produce a fine overall illumination, appropriately natural. The even illumination allows the children almost unlimited freedom of motion with no change in exposure calculation. With direct light, you must recalculate exposure with every shift in the light-to-subject distance. Bounce light used alone or in conjunction with existing room light is also less disrupting to children's normal activities. Before leaving the problems of photographing the older child, let's crush a universally held theory for calculating necessary shutter speeds to stop a child's actions. You have probably seen numerous charts carefully detailing the exact shutter speeds necessary for stopping various objects moving in specified directions—locomotives, automobiles, children. The shutter speed depends on whether the child, auto or train is moving toward, at a diagonal

Noon light is all right for youngsters: Overhead noon sunlight just doesn't seem to affect children as adversely as it does adults. Here the eye sockets are dark but certainly not objectionably so. Both portrait studies made with the 100mm f/3.5 Auto-Rokkor on the Minolta SR-2 were spur-of-the-moment pictures, shot quickly so the children would not freeze, become coy or act timid. Head of boy at right was deliberately abbreviated to center interest on boy at left. Exposure for both shots was about f/11 at 1/125 sec. Film was Kodak Plus-X.

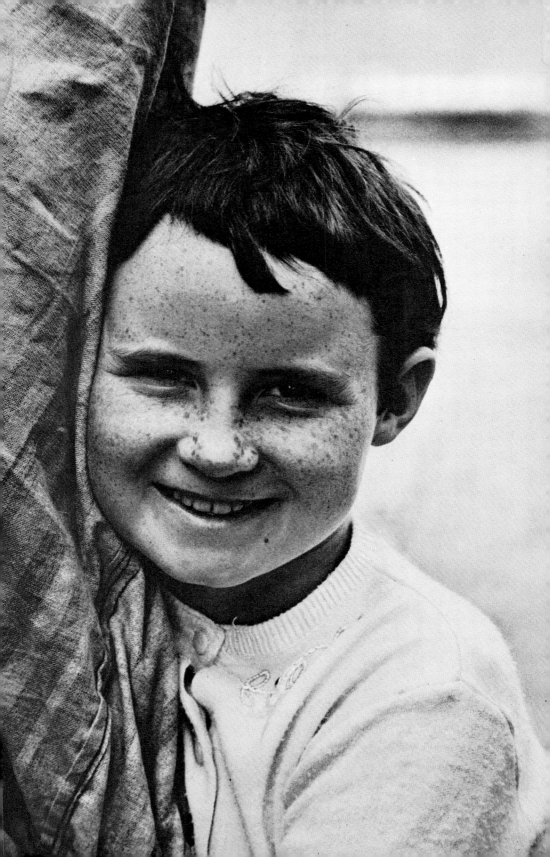

or at right angles to or away from the camera. In child photography this is all nonsense. While you may know where a car or train is going since the tracks and road do run in known directions, a child runs on neither rails nor roads. In addition, although the child may be travelling at a fairly easy-to-calculate speed, the arms and legs are actually pumping far faster than the total movement of the child. What speed should you use? The fastest possible under the lighting conditions.

Babies present special problems

We've been discussing the approach to ambulatory children, ranging in age from about three up. These are definitely a challenge. Babies, however, while not as tiring since they are more or less restricted to a specific area, present more acute problems. They neither walk, crawl nor sit. You can spend countless, frustrating hours attempting to elicit any expression whatsoever. Of course the average commercial baby photographer who can only spend a short time with each child has devised a system. The traditional propped up poses and artificial tricks of these photographers are so stereotyped I sometimes wonder why they don't shoot one set of pictures and merely print in different faces.

The challenge for a creative photographer is quite straightforward. The baby's photograph should reflect his or her personality, unformed and barely discernible though it may be. I had extreme misgivings about photographing my newly born daughter. Infants, I felt, were small packages of wants with little or no personality or attractiveness until they were a year old. This is untrue. Many babies are very photogenic at birth. Others, which do look a bit like a dried prune, recover within a week. Aside from the necessary and very unaesthetic first picture through the nursery glass, there are many excellent infant possibilities. They are very photogenic asleep, very photogenic in their mother's arms, and their feet and hands are photogenic.

Sharp detail is important

Oddly, I've found that one of the prime ingredients often necessary in pictures of infants is sharp detail. In baby pictures which have been inflicted upon me by proud fathers who were and were not good photographers, almost all have a singular lack of sharpness. Either fathers become nervous and can't hold a camera steady, or they feel there's really no detail on a baby—so why try? Technical carelessness is undoubtedly a factor. Since

Bounce flash for natural effects: Light bounced from a 10-foot high white ceiling by a Mighty Light Deluxe electronic flash unit furnished an exposure of f/11 for the 105mm f/2.5 Auto-Nikkor on my Nikon F. The film was Plus-X. During a lifetime of facing either my father's or my camera, my sister has become relatively immune to photography. I asked her to sit with daughter Kim on her lap, resting right below her chin. Then, while she conversed with my wife across the room, I made 15 shots. Note how essential the contrast in baby and adult skin texture is to the picture. As explained elsewhere, I regard the 100mm and 135mm lenses as fine focal lengths for close-up portraits.

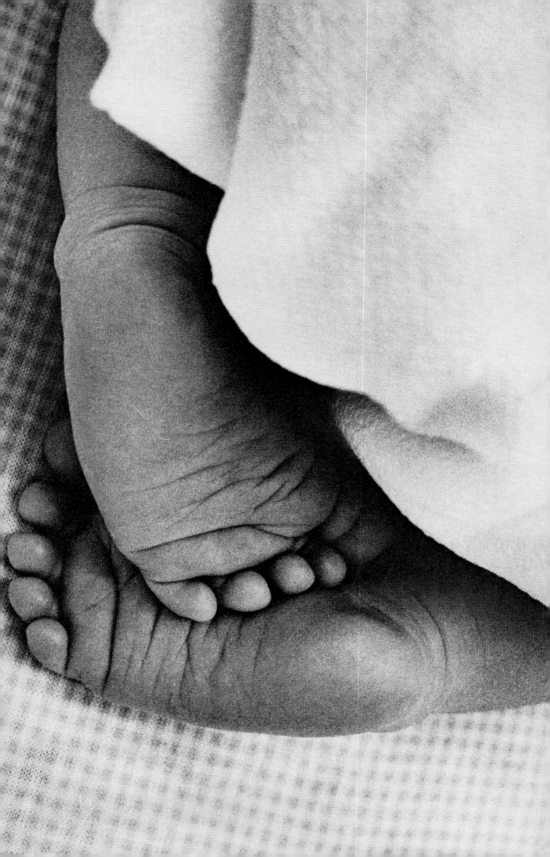

Find different angles for babies: All babies require is good technique plus a fresh approach. At left the close focusing 55mm f/1.8 Minolta Auto-Rokkor documents a typical infant position. Electronic flash light bounced from ceiling produced an exposure of f/5.6. Picture at right was made seconds later with same exposure. Effectiveness depends upon detail in skin and material. Although Minolta has no preview button, it was easy to check sharpness through the prism finder at f/5.6 before winding the film and thus recocking lens.

there is little real animation and the features, the body, and the arms are yet so unformed, you need all the technique you can apply so you won't lose what's there.

Pediatricians say that the light from direct flash plus moderate ten minute dosages of floods won't hurt a baby's eyes. Strong bounce flash or flood, however, delivers much more attractive light for baby photographs. Bounce flood is my personal favorite source. You can see exactly how this light affects the subject by simply checking through the prism finder. Important points to delineate clearly are ears, the fingers, feet, hair and, of course, the eyes. For contrast against the smooth skin, try to pick up the detail and texture in the child's clothes or bedding (see pictures, above and left).

Don't exert yourself trying to think up novel shooting solutions. Take them as they come in a child's day—feeding, bathing, sleeping, wakefulness. Examine each carefully for that slightly different expression or pose which marks one baby from another.

131

10

PRACTICAL
LOW
LIGHT
TECHNIQUES

Since the advent of 35mm photography, there has always existed a determined group of fanatics bent on proving that pictures can indeed be taken with little or no illumination. Recently we've emerged from another period of low light hysteria in which miracle developers, hypersensitized films, super-super speed lenses were used in various combinations to produce the most dreadful quality pictures imaginable.

There was some excuse for the low light rage. The fastest films until recent years had ASA indexes of 100 or 200. These contained a 2.5 to 4X overexposure safety factor so that the amateur with poor equipment would not possibly underexpose his picture. The haphazard corner drugstore photofinisher couldn't underdevelop it either. If the resulting negative was heavily overexposed as a result, it was printable and few amateurs enlarged their negatives sufficiently to notice the excessive graininess.

Beginning about 1936, a succession of new, very expensive developers with wild and woolly claims made their appearance. They directed you to double the speed of your film or triple its speed. All the photographer actually did was to overdevelop the highlights and drop the safety factor. But he quickly succumbed to the developer claims and became a wild enthusiast himself. Surprisingly, few photographers made comparison tests in standard developers. As recently as five years ago, a leading Eastman Kodak researcher remarked with some bitterness that sales of Kodak D-76 or Microdol could be increased a hundred-fold if it were more expensive, and came in a fancy bottle with all sorts of inflated claims.

Logically, a film can be made to reproduce only what its original sensitivity has been capable of recording. If a film does not record shadow detail, it cannot reproduce it later by any tricky development. There are but two ways of improving a low light situation and both must be done before the

How grainy is fastest film?: From the beginning of low light photography, fast films have been shown off with pictures taken by candlelight—but not at f/2.8 and 1/50 sec. as was this photograph on Kodak Royal-X Pan. The camera was an Exakta with 58mm f/2 Biotar, the occasion was dinner, and the exposure was obtained by rating the film at about E.I. 3200 and taking a reading from the shirt and sweater area. The graininess here is just about the limit I would tolerate in a print under any conditions.

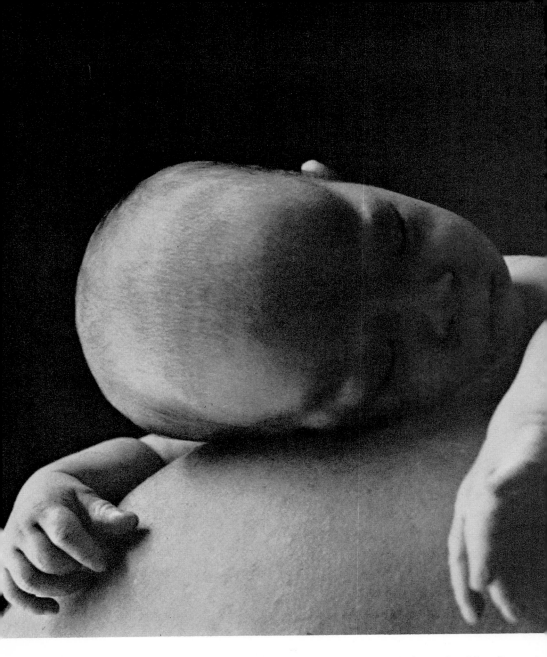

Even weak windowlight can do: The child lay on the father's shoulder illuminated solely by dying daylight seeping through a murky window. As usual, when visiting, I had a camera along but no film. Luckily the father had a roll of Super-XX (I think) and after he indicated where it was, I loaded the Exakta feverishly in hopes the child wouldn't wake up. Shooting at 1/25 sec. at f/2.8 with a 58mm f/2 Biotar, I polished off the entire roll of 36 exposures in about two minutes while the father turned around at various angles.

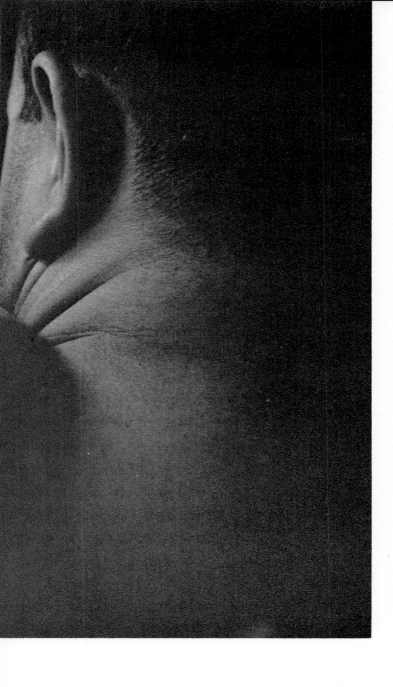

shutter release is pressed—increase the exposure or increase the illumination.

Today's Kodak Tri-X Pan with its 400 ASA index is capable of solving many low light problems. If you need a faster film try Agfa Isopan Record, which can be rated as high as 1600. Before long Kodak Royal-X Pan will undoubtedly make its appearance and it can easily be used at an exposure index of 3200 (picture, page 112). Develop according to the manufacturer's instructions (Agfa Rodinal for Record and DK-50 for Royal-X).

These ratings will produce excellent negatives quite capable of enlargement (with moderate graininess) to 11 x 14 provided you make your exposure meter readings carefully. Take the readings from the darkest area in which you want complete detail. If the detail is unimportant and you don't mind black, filled-in shadows you can take a reading from a lighter tone, even a highlight if nothing darker matters. What you are doing, in effect, is scientifically determining just what you wish recorded on the film and giving the minimum exposure for it.

Added speed is often illusory

Eastman Kodak does suggest that you can obtain even greater speed by increasing the index further and extending developing time. I find this speed to be largely illusory. You obtain a negative with denser highlights which may be easier to print but I fail to find more shadow detail in such a negative. Extended development increases graininess and contrast.

The secret of good technique is to keep exposure time to a minimum, developer time to a minimum but produce a negative printable on No. 2 or 3 contrast enlarging paper. Thin negatives caused by exceeding the exposure indexes will usually be printable only on a No. 4 or No. 5 contrast paper. These contrasts have a tendency to bring out the graininess far more than a No. 2 or 3.

With today's nicely cushioned shutters and instant return mirrors, hand-held speeds of ⅛, ¼ sec. can be used provided you know your subject material well enough to catch it at the opportune moment when such a speed will not result in a blur from motion. It will take some time to learn how to rest the camera securely against your forehead, steady it with both hands, place your feet in a secure but flexible position, hold your breath and squeeze off a shot as if you were firing a rifle. And you should learn how to do this automatically so you can concentrate on the subject. It's a big order but there's nothing quite as rewarding as low light shooting with Panatomic-X or Plus-X Pan. Low light pictures with little or no grain are a delight and rare as honest developer claims (see picture, opposite page).

Here are a few other low light tips I've learned from experience. No matter the maximum aperture of your lens, try to shoot at f/2.8 instead of f/2 or f/1.8. The difference in lens performance and the gain in depth of field makes it a well worthwhile goal.

Avoid medium toned objects which are out-of-focus. Graininess is always more apparent in out-of-focus subject material than sharp objects.

Whenever you can boost illumination by pulling aside curtains, turning Venetian blind slats to let in light, bringing a lamp closer, or moving your subject, do so.

Color photography in low light has received a shot in the exposure index

Slow film for low light?: Well, why not use Kodak Panatomic-X for low light photography if the subject is fairly motionless? I must confess that the Kodak Panatomic-X was very much in the nature of an experiment to see just how much quality can be squeezed from low light conditions. Photographer Maynard Frank Wolfe was examining pages in a magazine on my kitchen table while his wife, Edwina, stood behind him, leaning over his shoulder. Ordinary household lighting was used. Two 100-watt household lamps in paper reflector shades hung from the ceiling over the table center. A shot at f/2.8 and 1/8 sec. was made with the Minolta SR-2 and 55mm f/1.8 Auto-Rokkor, hand held. The resulting unposed double portrait looks more like a careful studio setup partially because of the lighting which seems so precise (and wasn't) and partially because of the very fine quality of the print thanks to Panatomic-X and proper development.

within recent years from the new superspeed color films. High Speed Ektachrome has an index of 160 outdoors and 125 under tungsten illumination. Super Anscochrome with an index of 100 is also much in the running. Many color processors will, if asked, alter processing so you can double these indexes. Color will not be so excellent or graininess so fine but results are certainly passable by professional standards. Higher indexes are hazardous. There is no way of increasing the speed of Kodachrome in processing. Negative color film indexes can often be doubled if there is no important deep shadow detail.

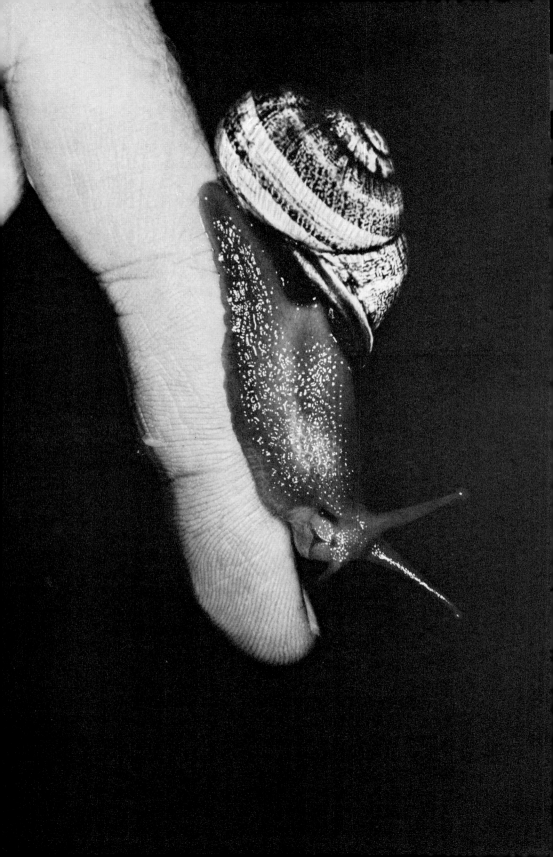

11

UNDER
YOUR
NOSE
AND
CLOSER

There's no greater revelation for a new eye-level reflex camera owner than to turn the focusing mount to its closest focusing distance—generally about 18 inches—and look through the prism finder. Here is a new world to photograph right under the camera's nose. With close-up lenses or extension tubes you can move in even further and there's practically no degree of magnification you can't reach with the proper lens combination. Certainly no other camera type can produce the close-up results possible with a single lens reflex.

For practical purposes, let's limit our discussion of close-up photography to that region not normally reachable by the rangefinder 35mm camera—from three feet downwards. We will eliminate from discussion photomicrography, since the entire subject of taking pictures through a microscope deserves a book by itself and I admit I've done relatively little in this field. However, I *have* done much experimentation this side of photomicrography—in macrophotography, which is the technique used in shooting close-ups without a microscope.

When you were a child did you ever take a cardboard tube, pretend it was a telescope, and look through it? Most children do this and suddenly find in looking through the glassless tube that there are things which they had scarcely noticed before. By excluding the overall view and concentrating on the tiny area within the tube, they brought their entire power of perception to bear on the small area.

This childhood technique can also be used to find suitable subject material for photography. Focus your camera at its nearest focusing point and

It's simple with a reflex: This Italian land snail was saved from entering a garlicky stewpot by my wife. Francis (Frances?) soon became a house pet living in a made-over, waterless glass aquarium and subsisting on the outer leaves of Romaine lettuce heads plus some carrot. His afternoon and evening strolls were taken up and down my wife's finger. Using a Miranda reflex, loaded with Panatomic-X film, I photographed the constitutional with a 135mm f/3.5 Schneider Tele-Xenar and +2 closeup lens. Light was supplied by a Mighty Light Electronic flash ringlight. The lens aperture was about f/11. While moderate strength close-up lenses can be used with excellent results, you need extension tubes or bellows for higher magnifications.

Close-ups without accessories: Each of these 11th and 12th century door panels found in Verona, Italy was more fascinating than the next. Commercial postcards of the entire doors were available but of very poor quality. Using the 55mm f/1.9 Steinheil Auto-Quinon lens on a Miranda, I first made overall pictures of the door panels on Plus-X film. Then, focusing the lens to 18 in. I documented each panel at f/16, 1/60 sec. The cross-lighting aided in showing up each detail. If I did it over again, however, I'd use Panatomic-X to achieve even finer detail.

examine details around your home through the prism finder by moving in towards your subject until it's sharp in the viewfinder. I must confess that my first fascination led me to ashtrays whose contents—ashes, lipstick-stained butts, burnt matches against the contours and decorations of the ashtray itself—proved overwhelmingly interesting. It would be untrue to say that each of these ashtrays yielded an outstanding picture, but they certainly were a wonderful start towards a new concept in close-up subjects. Next I began to examine parts of things. The texture of materials and their ornamentation—tapestry and embroidery for instance—became interesting little abstracts whose quality I could vary by simply changing the lighting. I examined the insides of a flower and found pure pattern. I began to find pictures within pictures. It was also good practice in learning to compose and create photographs. If you have paintings or reproductions of paintings, try your prism reflex on them, picking out a small portion of brushwork and color and making an individual abstract of it.

Perhaps you're wondering why I've stressed what to many might seem an esoteric side of the prism reflex. Actually, shooting ordinary subjects between 18 inches and 3 feet represents no problem. Whether you're dealing with a parakeet sitting on a friend's finger or shooting a close-up of a child sticking out its tongue at 18 in., the problem and technique are too simple to need explanation. You just focus, use the smallest aperture you can under the given lighting situations and then shoot.

141

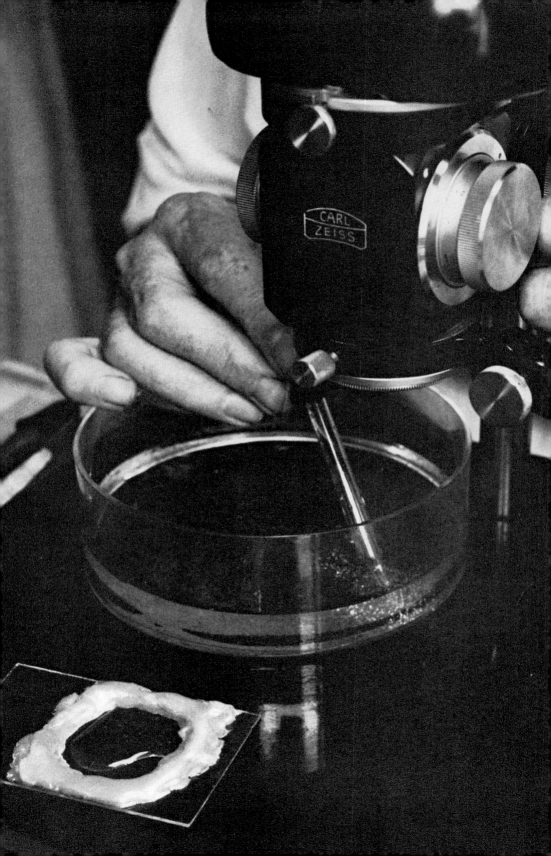

If we were discussing how to take such pictures with a rangefinder camera you might need much more involved technical explanations on how to go about doing it, but the eye-level reflex makes such close-ups so simple that there's little sense in discussing them. Once you've turned your focusing ring as far as it will go and still not achieved great enough image size, or gotten close enough to your subject, your technical troubles begin. If you own a leaf shutter reflex you must start using close-up lenses. If you have a focal plane shutter reflex, you can either rely on close-up lenses in addition to your normal lens or extension tubes or bellows between the lens and your camera.

The great close-up conflict—extension tubes and bellows vs. supplementary lenses—has always left photographers in a dilemma. Leaf shutter single-lens reflex owners have no choice and therefore no dilemma. Because of the camera and shutter construction, extension tubes or bellows cannot be used. If you have a focal plane shutter reflex, however, is it worth the trouble to use an extension? The lens must be removed from the camera, the extension inserted and then the necessary exposure increase must be calculated. In addition, since you're working with a single-lens reflex, any extension tube between the lens and camera interrupts the automatic diaphragm mechanism and you must shut the lens down manually to the proper opening—or use a double cable release (see pictures, page 153).

All is sunny and joyful if you use close-up lenses—or is it? Just slip one over your lens and shoot. You need no exposure increase, your automatic diaphragm lens will work as always. But someone will say darkly, "Close-up lenses cause distortion, they are limited, they entail a distinct loss of definition in the picture." Well, do they?

Instead of throwing a lot of theoretical truths at you, I undertook a series of extensive tests using standard camera lenses so that I could obtain practical working criteria on the extension vs. close-up lens battle as it affects most of us. Let's start with the simple technique first—adding the close-up lens.

The close-up lens, when added to your camera lens, shortens the effective focal length of the combination. In doing so, it produces the equivalent of a slightly shorter focal-length lens on an extension. The stronger the close-up lens, the shorter the effective focal length. For instance, a 50mm lens with a +1 becomes 47.6mm; with a +2, 45.9mm; with a +3, 42.9mm, and so on all the way up to the strongest close-up lens in general use today, the +10, which with a 50mm lens makes 33.4mm. With the +10 lens you can produce an image on film about $\frac{8}{10}$ size of your actual subject. If you want

Indoor close-up using daylight: Here's a type of photograph that's about impossible to shoot with a rangefinder 35mm camera unless you own the most complicated and costly accessory equipment. With an eye-level reflex, it's easy. Microbiologist Roman Vishniac was working close to a window in his laboratory at the Oceanographic Institute in Woods Hole, Mass. He was transferring tiny marine creatures from the large bowl into the wax lake on the glass slide in the foreground which he put under his microscope for study. I found a chair, took it outside, stood on it and peered in the window. With the 55mm f/1.8 Auto-Rokkor lens of the Minolta SR-2 camera focused at its closest point, I made this exposure at f/11, 1/30 sec. on Plus-X film.

a larger image (more magnification) you must use a longer focal-length lens (see illustration, page 148). A 200mm lens when used with a +10 loses effective focal length and produces the effect of a 66.6mm. You can see what actually happens in the illustration on page 147.

What are the limitations? Why can't you use a long lens and a +10 or stronger close-up lens and get all the magnification you want?

Unfortunately, as the close-up lens gets stronger and the camera lens longer in focal length, picture definition decreases. Some manufacturers have stated that a +5 close-up lens on a 50mm camera lens is the strongest combination possible before definition is affected noticeably. In our tests we found that the strongest combination used by most amateurs, a 50mm lens with a +3 close-up lens, produced images of a quality indistinguishable from an image of the same size produced by using an extension (see illustrations, opposite), *provided the 50mm lens was set at a small aperture when used with the close-up lens.*

Lenses which normally produce good results at large apertures may not produce images of equal quality when used with close-up lenses. They must be stopped down. How far? Frankly it depends on the quality and optical construction of your camera lens. As far as definition is concerned, the better the camera lens the less you need stop down when using close-up lenses. As you use longer and longer lenses to get bigger and bigger images, definition falls off noticeably because the average long lens used on 35mm cameras is designed for distance work and is corrected accordingly. It's difficult to point to the exact limit of tolerable definition loss, but in my opinion a 135mm f/3.5 lens used at f/5.6 with a +3 close-up lens (effective focal length 96mm) is about the maximum allowable focal length and close-up lens limit before definition is affected. This combination can produce a 35mm negative capable of enlargement to 11 x 14. If you have lower goals, you can perhaps go further in close-up lenses, focal lengths or larger apertures.

Besides the increasing loss of definition, the loss of effective focal length has unpleasant consequences. While it may not seem too much to cut back to a 47.6mm effective focal length when using a +1 lens on a 50mm camera lens, the idea of reducing a 200mm lens to 66.6mm with a +10 is quite appalling. The close-up lens, by reducing the effective focal length, cancels out one of the principal reasons for using a long lens for close-up work— minimizing perspective distortion. The predominant foreground, such as an insect's head, can become overly large in relationship to the body. So, close-up lenses of moderate strength will behave nicely on long lenses for portraits and the like. For extreme close-up work with strong close-up lenses, you will run into definition and perspective distortion problems with all lenses.

Lastly, close-up lenses severely limit the distance you can put between yourself and your subject. The strength of the close-up lens alone determines how far away you will be from the subject (see illustration, page 147). With

Extension or close-up lens?: I've often been asked how much sharpness is lost when an object is photographed through a close-up lens as compared to the same photograph made by using extension tubes or bellows. Here's a graphic illustration of what you can and what you can't do if you wish to achieve the best results with your eye level reflex when shooting finely detailed subjects.

HOW SHARP ARE THE RESULTS FROM A +3 LENS?

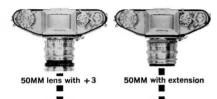

50MM lens with +3   50MM with extension

full negative   full negative

HOW SHARP ARE THE RESULTS FROM A +10 LENS?

50MM lens with +10   50MM with extension

full negative   full negative

8X enlargement of wing is sharp and clear

8X enlargement of wing is sharp and clear

8X enlargement of wing is sharp and clear

8X enlargement of wing shows definition loss

a +1 and your lens at infinity, you must be no further than 39.37 in. from your subject. With a +2 you must be no more than 19.6 in. from the subject, with a +3 no more than 13.2 in. With a +10 you'll be only 3.93 in. away. It's obvious that candid portrait photography is out when you're using a close-up lens, since you'll be right on top of your subject.

By now it should be fairly obvious that you're paying a heavy optical penalty for the ease of using the close-up lens. And the larger the image you intend to produce, the larger the penalty.

It's well worth going to the trouble of using the extension tube or bellows if your camera has a focal-plane shutter. Most of the problems produced by close-up lenses are avoided:

1. As far as results are concerned, extending the lens away from the camera body is the best way to insure top quality close-ups.

2. There is no theoretical limit to the magnification possible with extension. Extend the lens further and you get more magnification (see illustration, opposite).

3. You can lessen perspective distortion with a longer lens, since the focal length of your lens does not change when you're using it with extension.

4. The longer the lens, the further away you can be from your subject while obtaining the same size image. (You can see it on opposite page.)

The major problem is the loss of lens speed caused by increasing the lens-to-film-plane distance. How much speed do you lose? If you use a 50mm lens and stop it down to f/16, and you want to make a close-up in which the image on the film will be life size (1:1), the effective aperture will become f/32. The effective aperture will become smaller as the image size you wish to produce on the film becomes greater.

It would therefore seem intelligent to shoot with your camera lens wide open to take full advantage of your speed. However, there is a snag here. Even the best of lenses won't deliver maximum definition (which you particularly need for close-ups) at full aperture. Thus for maximum definition, always close down at least one stop from the widest aperture if you're using a moderate speed lens (for an f/3.5 lens, stop down to f/5.6) or three stops if you're using a high-speed lens (for an f/2 lens, to f/5.6). Moreover, this loss of effective aperture when using extensions also drastically curtails the amount of illumination reaching the ground glass of reflex cameras and housings. While this has been solved to some extent in scientific instruments by inserting split prisms in the viewing system, the magnification possible with a ground-glass or reflex prism viewing system is limited by the amount of illumination falling on the subject and the brilliance of the ground glass.

Bellows or close-up lenses, what are the differences? Here's a graphic illustration depicting them. Note that the close-up lens requires an extremely close approach to the subject no matter the lens used while the extension permits you to get quite far away. Also note how drastically the focal length of the camera lens is altered when a close-up lens is used and how this affects the apparent perspective of the three dice. The loss in definition with a long camera lens and close-up accessory lens is noticeable. Conclusion: although the close-up lens is more convenient for exposure computation, an extension will generally yield better results.

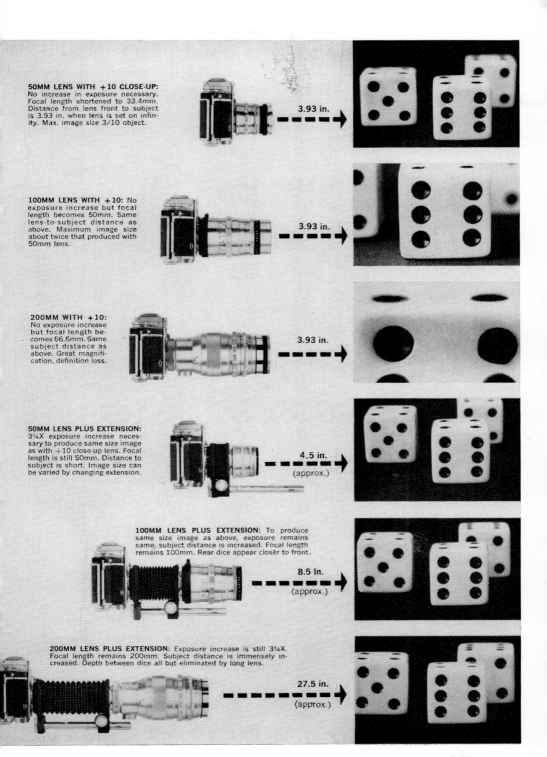

50MM LENS WITH +10 CLOSE-UP: No increase in exposure necessary. Focal length shortened to 33.4mm. Distance from lens front to subject is 3.93 in. when lens is set on infinity. Max. image size 3/10 object.

3.93 in. →

100MM LENS WITH +10: No exposure increase but focal length becomes 50mm. Same lens-to-subject distance as above. Maximum image size about twice that produced with 50mm lens.

3.93 in. →

200MM WITH +10: No exposure increase but focal length becomes 66.6mm. Same subject distance as above. Great magnification, definition loss.

3.93 in. →

50MM LENS PLUS EXTENSION: 3¼X exposure increase necessary to produce same size image as with +10 close-up lens. Focal length is still 50mm. Distance to subject is short. Image size can be varied by changing extension.

4.5 in. →
(approx.)

100MM LENS PLUS EXTENSION: To produce same size image as above, exposure remains same, subject distance is increased. Focal length remains 100mm. Rear dice appear closer to front.

8.5 in. →
(approx.)

200MM LENS PLUS EXTENSION: Exposure increase is still 3¼X. Focal length remains 200mm. Subject distance is immensely increased. Depth between dice all but eliminated by long lens.

27.5 in. →
(approx.)

147

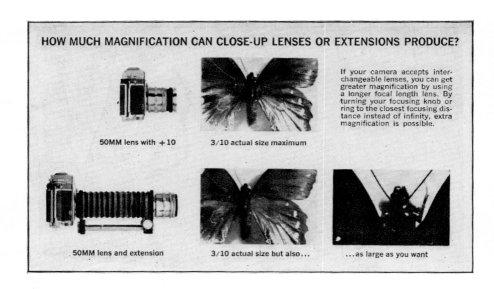

HOW MUCH MAGNIFICATION CAN CLOSE-UP LENSES OR EXTENSIONS PRODUCE?

If your camera accepts inter-changeable lenses, you can get greater magnification by using a longer focal length lens. By turning your focusing knob or ring to the closest focusing dis-tance instead of infinity, extra magnification is possible.

50MM lens with +10

3/10 actual size maximum

50MM lens and extension

3/10 actual size but also...

...as large as you want

How are you going to determine your effective aperture? Although we could give you a formula, the Kodak Master Photo Guide ($1.75) contains an effective aperture computer, and this is far easier and handier to use. It also contains a second method of achieving the right exposure, advising you how much additional exposure will be needed for the amount of exten-sion you are using. Incidentally, many bellows units contain exposure scales right on their tracks. It's something well worth looking for when you're shopping for a bellows unit. A full instruction pamphlet with exposure sug-gestions should accompany any extension tubes you buy.

This still leaves you with the problem of stopping down that lens manually after you've focused. The new Praktica extension tubes have an internal mechanism which allows complete automatic operation with the tubes. Other manufacturers of reflexes have promised similar units, but they've been promising them for a long time.

Since depth of field is an important aspect of all close-up work, you may be wondering why we haven't discussed the depth of field available with close-up lenses as opposed to that available with extension. The reason is this: depth of field is solely a function of magnification. The larger the image size on the negative (regardless of how it got there) the less depth of field there is at any given aperture. There's only one way of increasing depth of field—close down your lens.

Briefly, summing up, the loss of definition from close-up lenses has been vastly exaggerated. They're fine in moderate strength with moderate focal-length lenses. For extreme close-ups, use tubes or a bellows unit.

Bellows units, I feel, are preferable to extension tubes because they can be racked back and forth to the exact focus and magnification wanted in a matter of seconds. There is no reason why you can't get started with one of the less expensive lightweight units in the $10 to $15 range.

I use a 135mm lens for most close-up work. I preferred the 135mm length to the normal from the very first minute I discovered how close I must get to a hornet to photograph him with a 50mm lens. (Hornets are pretty in Kodachrome, but keep at least a 135mm lens between you and them). Butterflies, too, reacted more favorably to the greater camera-to-subject distance possible with a 135mm lens. In addition, the 135mm length allowed us to light our subjects easily without the lens in the way.

If you intend to do any close-up work using active subjects, you'll want to trigger the automatic diaphragm of the lens just before the shutter goes off. You'll need a double cable release and an automatic lens with a cable release socket. Get an inexpensive double release which has provision for adjustment of the two cables so they can be synchronized with the shutter.

There are many excellent inexpensive copying stands. If you have an enlarger with vertical center post you can save the price of a stand by using the Accura Universal Copy Bracket which has a camera platform attached.

The advantage of the entire rig is that you can use camera, bellows, lens and cable release on the copying stand indoors (see page 153), or remove the combination and hand-hold outdoor shots. For more exacting work you can thread the unit to a tripod. The tripod should have a center pole which can be removed and inverted, allowing you to get the camera right down to ground level when necessary. Of course the camera will be upside down and you will have to shoot with an eye-level prism rather than the waist-level finder.

You would expect that the best and simplest place to shoot outdoor close-ups would be outdoors. It isn't. At least not for beginners. Naturally, hornets, live butterflies and trees stay outdoors. But you have three difficult outdoor problems—background, lighting and exposure.

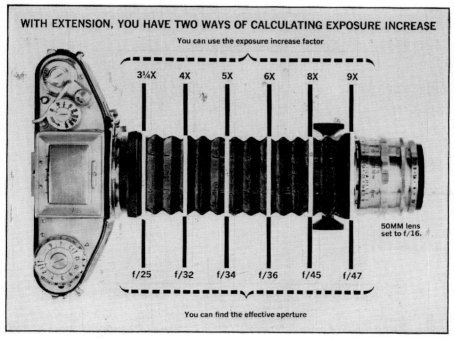

WITH EXTENSION, YOU HAVE TWO WAYS OF CALCULATING EXPOSURE INCREASE

You can use the exposure increase factor

3¼X   4X   5X   6X   8X   9X

50MM lens set to f/16.

f/25   f/32   f/34   f/36   f/45   f/47

You can find the effective aperture

Background: Most small earth creatures are camouflage experts, and unless they are creeping, crawling or resting against a rather contrasting uncluttered background, the results will be confusing.

Lighting: As you extend your bellows, your effective lens opening decreases, requiring a great deal more exposure as we've seen. While reflectors including concave mirrors can help somewhat, subjects often prefer shady nooks. Electronic flash, with its possibility of creating double images when used at $\frac{1}{25}$ to $\frac{1}{60}$ sec., can be more of a hindrance than a help.

Exposure: A ground mite making the bug's equivalent of a 500-yard dash to clear out of your way is not stopped at $\frac{1}{5}$ sec. You need fast shutter speeds. With daylight, you may or may not get sufficient lighting for $\frac{1}{125}$ sec. or faster speeds.

Indoors we had the following advantages:

Background: Bring it indoors with you. Put your subjects in a small plastic container with the background, and instead of moving the camera to keep the insect or what-have-you in focus, move the container. Don't mix your insect with impossible backgrounds—a millipede crawling over a damask table cloth. Instead, use something a millipede might actually crawl across—a leaf, for instance, or a piece of white quartz. Pick backgrounds with fairly even surfaces so that your camera won't need refocusing constantly as the insect moves about.

Lighting: Floods will fry most little creatures if you keep the lights on while you're focusing and arranging your picture. Instead, get your indoor-outdoor studio set up fairly close to a window. You can view and focus by windowlight and only turn on the floods when necessary. If you are going to do a great deal of close-up work, a ringlight electronic flash unit produces

Check your focus: If you don't use a reflex, this type of double portrait's just about an impossibility. Through the prism of the Exakta with 58mm f/2 Biotar I was able to frame the two heads exactly and then check the sharpness of each head. I switched focus several times from rear to front head and shot several pictures with one in focus and then the other. The film was Plus-X, exposure about f/16 at 1/50 on a bright sunny afternoon.

You can hand-hold for super close-ups: It was obvious that this Japanese beetle wouldn't wait for me to set up a tripod. It was equally clear that I couldn't use a close-up lens. If I did, I'd have to come too close and away would go the beetle. I settled for a Miranda and 135mm f/3.5 Schneider Tele-Xenar lens plus a bellows unit. Using a double cable release to activate the automatic diaphragm in conjunction with the shutter of the camera, I made an exposure at f/16 and 1/60 sec. on Plus-X holding the camera bellows and lens in my hand.

Left: To make close-ups using extension tubes and bellows units easier, new tubes are being developed which feature internal automatic connections between camera body and lens. This unit uses spring-operated pushrod.

Center: An alternative to the internally coupled extension tube is the double cable release and activating collar. The collar, operated by one of the cables, works the automatic diaphragm of the lens while other trips shutter.

Right: Here's an economical close-up arrangement. A copying stand with flexible gooseneck flood reflectors holds a reflex with waist-level finder. A bellows unit, 135mm lens and double cable release complete the system.

good overall illumination even if it is characteristically lacking in shadows.

Exposure: Before you put your insect down under the camera, take a meter reading. We've found that an incident reading meter is handier since it's difficult to take a proper reading from a subject whose total area may not occupy more than 10 percent of a reflecting meter's angle of coverage. With floors or electronic flash you should be able to build up enough light for just about any animal and speed.

So far I haven't mentioned copying as a part of close-up photography. Actually, if you can learn to shoot living creatures successfully, you can copy documents, drawings or photographs practically with your eyes closed.

The close-up stand we've already discussed will do nicely although for most copying work you'll actually be able to hand-hold some shots. Simply lay the material to be copied flat on the stand base, lower the camera to whatever height is necessary to get the biggest image on the prism glass, focus and fire away. I've found that overcast sunlight, bright shade or windowlight is splendidly even for copy work. Floods can be tricky since they can cause reflections on glossy material. Of course, you'll be able to see this immediately through the prism finder. Use a fine-grained film, (if it's black and white), or Kodachrome if you want color. For line copying or book type try Micro-File film.

If your main interest in close-up shooting is copy work you can simplify your camera equipment. You certainly won't need the double cable release mentioned. Your normal camera lens on a bellows will perform splendidly. Focus wide open, shut the lens down to the proper aperture, then shoot.

One word of warning. If you're shooting on color film, you'll probably want to fill the transparency or color negative completely with the material

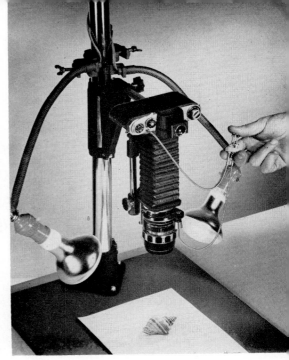

to be copied. In color, whatever the camera sees will be on the transparency. Unfortunately, this isn't entirely true for the viewfinder. Most prism finders show slightly less than the total area actually committed to film. If exact area is important to you, run a test roll through your camera first. A newspaper page pinned to a wall is an excellent target to check the discrepancy (if any) between your viewfinder and the camera.

The field of close-up photography is a large one and the single-lens reflex is ideally fitted for it. While most of us will be using our regular camera lenses as we've already discussed, special lenses and special techniques with regular camera lenses do exist.

For extreme close-up work using bellows attachments, there are special macro lenses of 25mm focal length or less made by Schneider and Zeiss which you might want to investigate. Some close-up photographers do claim sharper pictures by reversing the lens and fastening the lens front closest to the camera body. There are special lens attachments for this but frankly, I've been perfectly satisfied with my lenses used in the normal position.

12

MY PET
CURES
AND
POISONS

While we've covered a good deal of ground in eye-level reflex mechanical techniques, in equipment and in approaches to the subjects, there are loose ends, sundry hints, last minute reminders and short cuts that have somehow been neglected. Herewith I take pot shots at them in and out of order, hoping that none are forgotten.

Camera cleaning: Eye-level reflexes get dirtier and do it more quickly than do any other types of cameras. While a speck of dust or grit on the mirror or bottom of the prism housing may not affect the picture, the resulting spot seen in the finder will drive you slowly mad. Reflex housings which are removable must be taken off and, if the ground glass inset is removable, it too must be separated. A soft brush will eliminate small lint pieces, hairs and similar oddities. Some brushes I've purchased, however, seem to be made from a bristle which is oily by nature. Try the brush out first before using it on your photo equipment. A brush with a small air syringe can blow dust particles out of nooks and crannies. Don't use your breath. It's loaded with too much moisture. When cleaning always hold whatever you're working on upside down and clean from underneath so gravity can rid you of the dust, or, like a bad housewife, you'll just be stirring the dust which will then settle on your camera elsewhere.

Be careful of that mirror!

Mirrors inside reflexes are very delicate since the silver coating is at the front and not behind the glass. The brush can flick off dust spots. The only perfect remedy for fingerprints—don't get any on in the first place. I know no sure way of removing them from the mirror. Sometimes you can remove a light fingerprint by breathing on a folded lens tissue and gently rubbing the spot with the tip.

To clean a lens properly, which won't respond to the brush alone, fold a piece of lens tissue sufficiently so that you can just barely tear it in half. After tearing it, hold the untorn end in your fingers and rub the torn end over the lens in a circular motion outwards, starting from the center. Using this method, you won't bring too much pressure to bear on the lens surface (pictures, pages 158 and 159). In the absence of lens tissue, use Kleenex. This is equally as good as lens tissues but will leave some lint which can be removed by the brush. Never use silicone-treated eyeglass tissues. They may damage either the lens or the lens coating.

Sometimes the view through the finder will appear quite hazy. This is often caused by oil from eyelashes distributing itself on the rear eyepiece of the finder. You can use a clean handkerchief or other soft cloth to remove the oil, since the finder glass is not as delicate as the lens.

Mount tightening: It's safe to tighten only the Exakta and Miranda type lens mount. Others need a professional repairman. If you own a reflex with an Exakta mount and the lens seems loose, insert a fine blade in the three narrow slits located in the inner circumference of the lens mount of the camera. Simply widen the three slits lightly and the lens will become tight when you reinsert it.

Jamming: Most jammed cameras must be fixed by repairmen. However, if you have a camera with a rapid return mirror which jams in the "up" position, you can often free it by removing the lens and drawing the mirror downwards with the tip of a fingernail. Be careful not to fingerprint the mirror. Now let go of the mirror and try to press the shutter release or wind the film. If this doesn't release the jam, try this last remedy before heading into the repair shop: with your fingernail, try to catch one of the edges of the focal plane shutter. Draw it gently about half way across the focal plane and let it return with a snap. Failing this, try no more.

Repairs: where and when

Repairs: There are many camera butchers. If possible have your camera returned to the importer. Each importer maintains a factory-authorized repair agency which, while very slow (sometimes a repair can take six weeks), is reliable.

If a repairman claims to be an authorized repair agency, drop the camera importer a note asking if this is so. Often it isn't.

Speedy service is at a premium. Professional photographers whose livings depend on cameras do get preferential treatment. There are, however, a few excellent non-factory repair agencies throughout the country who cater to professional photographers. Call up the leading professional photographers in your own town and ask them who the professional repairman is. In New York it's Professional Camera Repair Service. Sometimes such an outfit may do your repair if they're not busy overhauling cameras for the National Geographic Magazine staff or Life magazine staff. Oddly, prices are exceedingly moderate.

Maintenance: Your camera does not need cleaning and oiling once a year, once every two years or even every five years. It will need exercise at all shutter speeds and apertures every week if you don't use it constantly. Slow speeds and automatic diaphragms can become sluggish if not employed regularly. If you want to give your camera the same cleaning as a repairman can, attach the narrowest appliance to the blower end of a clean household vacuum cleaner and work the camera over inside and out.

While your camera does not need professional cleaning and oiling, it may need realignment. Check alignment every six months as outlined on page 53. The test will quickly indicate whether the mirror, the one alignment weak spot within the body, is coming to rest in the proper plane. If it doesn't, your focus will be off. Only a repairman can realign a mirror properly.

Carrying cameras: I have at one time owned and used every known method of carrying an eye-level reflex from point A to point B. As a result, I've formed strong likes and dislikes. I dislike all ever-ready cases, particularly the hard leather ones with the fronts which snap off or swivel. By the time you attempt to unbutton, unhook and find a resting place for the case front you have no subject. The new soft leather ever-ready cases available for some reflexes are a vast improvement but still awkward. The only serviceable way to carry a camera is without a case. First find a good carrying strap which will attach directly to the two eyelets on the camera body. After examining all sorts, I've found that almost all the commercial brands are not only unserviceable but may actually cause damage to your camera. Most have spring-loaded snap fasteners at the end. The fasteners are generally attached to swivels. The only device holding the swivel in place is often a small metal pin with a largish head sticking through a tiny stem. If the head should shear off, and I've seen it happen, away goes strap and camera. In addition the snap fasteners rub against the metal finish of the camera body scratching and often denting it. The only completely satisfactory camera strap I've found is the Bob Schwalberg strap, a tough heavier-than-usual leather strap with two metal split rings which fit the camera eyelets. There is no pinhead to snap off and only leather will come into contact with your camera body. In addition the middle of the strap sports a heavy snap lock

Far left: The small, snap open hard-side gadget bag with interchangeable interior compartments hold an astonishing collection which can be removed quickly. Here, two prism reflexes, three lenses, meter and loads of film slip neatly into place.

Center: Instead of carrying your case with the snap opening pointing outward, reverse it so the case opens inwards. You'll find it easier to remove equipment. The top also offers protection against inclement weather.

Left: Going by air? Take your tiny case, load it into an expandable plastic case which can also hold all your heavy non-photographable items. Airlines seldom weigh camera cases within reasonable size. When you arrive, remove small case, load with just the equipment and film you need.

which allows you to carry the camera over your shoulder underneath a coat. You can remove the camera without removing the coat which is often a handy trick. The strap is available from The Strapateer, 1335 South Ivanhoe Way, Denver 22, Col. There is no substitute.

While carrying the camera, keep the strap short so that the camera literally hangs underneath your armpit when the strap is over your shoulder. Your arm can protect it. Then, if you swing around suddenly there is no danger that the centrifugal force will send camera crashing against a wall.

A good gadget bag is a must. At some time in the life of every photographic fan, he or she thinks of the ideal answer. A huge gadget bag of beautiful leather quite capable of holding everything—with room for a few items yet unbought. It's a great idea until you try to lift the full bag from the ground. No funnier sight exists in a distant land than the American tourist gamely staggering under the weight of a giant camera case. And if you intend to take candids, the large case will announce your intentions louder than a fire siren. "Here comes the American and his camera case" or, if the case be of sufficient size, "here comes the case and its American."

What to do about it? Well, you can leave the big case at home or hotel and go off with reflex in hand plus a meter stuck in one pocket, rolls of film in another. You'll look sorta lumpy. And it's often rather difficult to extract that meter from your left rear pocket (if you're a man). Let's not mention

the possibility of sitting on it by error. Well anyway, the big case by itself doesn't really work out too well in practice.

In the course of two trips to Europe, ten days in the Caribbean and some fast weekends and day trips here and there, I think I now have the problem solved in a manner quite possible and practical for anyone.

Plan on taking your important cameras and equipment in one, small compact case. I've found that cases similar to that shown on pages 156 and 157 hold an unbelievable amount in a tiny, highly portable space. In the case seen, which is only 9½ x 4¼ x 5¾ in., I can carry one large eye-level reflex with a 50mm lens, another with a 135 or 105mm lens, plenty of film (six to eight rolls) a lens brush and lens tissue.

On the subject of small cases, I am against the zipper case and very much for the single snap top case (see photo). Zippers are a trial, no matter where placed. I always seem to get an exposure meter cord or something else caught in them, thereby jamming the case neither open nor closed. With the snap top case, I can turn the opening edge towards me and reach in for a piece of equipment in hot sun, rain or snow without letting the equipment inside suffer.

The new snap cases with interchangeable compartments, which you can change to suit your own needs, seemed like an excellent idea and have proved so, for me, anyhow.

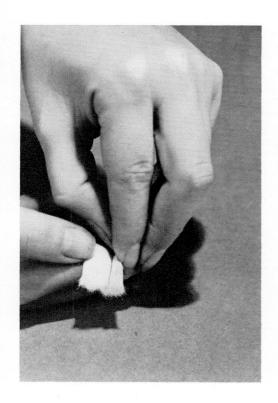

How to clean a lens: If you follow the practices of most photographers and fold the lens tissue into a little pad, then rub the surface of the lens with it, you are doing little save grinding the grit right into the glass. Instead, fold a sheet of lens tissue four or five times *(far left)*. Then tear folded sheet in middle *(center)*. Place two folded halves with torn edges together and roll into a small brush *(left)*. Use this brush to clean lens surface with circular motion starting at center and working outwards. By using flexibility of tissue and not applying pressure directly to surface you avoid lens damage—and you get a cleaner lens too!

Of course, this rather small case will probably not hold all you possess or even all you wish to take on a long trip. Pack all the rest of the film, extra lenses and what have you in with your regular luggage. Keep your working bag small and neat.

For the air traveler who will probably object to packing anything in his luggage which might send him closer to that 44-pound baggage limitation, I have a solution. It may sound really mad, but it works. I take my small case and place it inside a larger expandable plastic gadget bag. The reason: when you travel by air, the airlines seldom weigh your camera case unless you ask them to. Ergo, I load the big bag with my small camera case plus all the small objects—electric razors—etc., which are heavy and might send me over the 44-pound limit. When I arrive at my destination, I use the small bag for camera equipment while the large one remains in the hotel room collecting all the souvenirs I might pick up. Before leaving again for home, I can mail the souvenirs, put the small case within the large one and go home. It's wild, but it works.

Carrying film: When you buy film in cartridges, don't leave it in the little cardboard boxes until the moment you're ready to shoot or you'll regret it. Trying to extract a cartridge from the box, unwrap the foil and find a place to throw the trash while loading the camera, is arduous and time-consuming work. Those rectangular cardboard boxes also waste space. In

Europe the cartridges are packed in smaller boxes with a minimum of garbage. Here, however, all boxes are about the same large size, even the European films planned for export. After all, every film must fit the dealer's existing racks.

Unpack the film when you get it. If a metal container is furnished with the film, throw away everything but the container and place the naked cartridge within it. You can mark the outside of the can with a grease pencil to indicate the film type.

Kodak does not furnish cans with their black-and-white films. I've missed more than one picture in vain attempts to tear open the plastic envelopes. I've scrounged containers from all sorts of different films into which I could put the Kodak cartridges. Such frustrations led me to an excellent substitute for all containers—aluminum kitchen foil. Tear off a small rectangle of foil, roll up the cartridge and crimp the ends. You can grease mark the foil if you want to identify the films. Since one side of the foil is fairly shiny and the other side dull, to identify exposed from unexposed films, I wrap all unexposed film shiny side out and simply reverse the paper when rewrapping after exposure. You'll find the foil-wrapped cartridges are small, neat, and if wrapped tightly, fairly impervious to moisture.

Film filing: I see no reason to mount color transparencies in glass unless you intend to exhibit them in shows where other people will be handling or manhandling them. Professional photographers leave them in the cardboard mounts as they are returned from the processor. If you have an automatic projector, and I can hardly imagine color enthusiasts without them, store your transparencies in the interchangeable slide trays. If you don't own such a projector, keep the slides in the processors' plastic or cardboard boxes. Mark each slide so you will know the right facing and top side for viewing. And get a small rubber stamp with your name on it and mark each slide so no one can ever get your slides confused with other peoples'.

Keeping your black and whites straight

Black-and-white negatives and prints are more difficult to file, I think. I store my negatives, six in a strip, in glassine sleeves—not the completely transparent type in which the negatives sometimes stick—but the translucent kind. The six strips should be fitted into a flat cardboard sleeve. If your dealer has nothing like this, write the Nega-File Co., P.O. Box 405, Doylestown, Pa. for a catalog of their filing materials.

Instead of letting your negatives sit around with no proof positive of what pictures are on them, have made or make a glossy contact proof made of each roll of film (as illustrated on page 78) and keep the proofs in a loose leaf notebook with full data on the back as to the dates and places shown therein. Also jot down the number of the negative file where you can lay your hands on the original negative.

In such a book you can quickly find most individual pictures when you wish by glancing through the pages. You can then locate the negative and have a print made. While this may seem slightly less sure than a complete cross-indexed cardfile, the latter is a dream which even the most astute of professionals dares not attempt without a full time file clerk.

The contact sheet incidentally, is a great money and time saver. Over the years I've preferred them to jumbo prints. I can get just as great a kick from examining the tiny contacts with a magnifier as I can by looking at jumbo prints. A good flashlight magnifier is inexpensive and essential to a contact sheet file.

How to work from a contact sheet

You can also use the contact sheet for checking frames to be enlarged and for doing preliminary cropping with a red grease pencil. Don't depend on the contact sheet to check negative sharpness. Contact prints seldom are as sharp as the negatives. You can examine negatives with the same magnifier you've used for looking at the contact prints. Later you may want a smaller, more powerful magnifier. To examine a negative properly, hold it over a sheet of white paper on which a bright, even light is shining. Never try to look at a negative while holding it up to the light. A bright light behind will give a false impression of the density, shadow and highlight detail and graininess.

Prism brightness: There have been many devices and suggestions for all who desire a brighter ground glass focusing image. At one time, it was recommended that you spread a thin layer of vaseline on the underside of the ground glass. It did brighten the prism but made finding the exact point of maximum sharpness that much more difficult to determine. Only the Exakta ground glass was ever markedly improved by non-factory methods. A special ground-glass insert fitting inside the prism housing called a Lumlite, available from Aetna-Optix, 350 West 31st St., New York, N.Y. does produce a brighter and easier-to-focus image for normal and longer than normal focal length lenses. It doesn't seem to work well with wide angle lenses.

Beware of interchangeable prisms not made by the manufacturer of the camera. Bargains are poor investments and have always shown up as inferior in quality when I've tested them.

And some tripods are dreadful

Tripods: Except for steadying ⅛ and ¹⁄₁₅ sec. hand-held shots, a telescoping tube tripod is virtually useless no matter how lovely it may be to look at. A good tripod must be steady, high enough to use at eye-level, have provision for locking the three legs in an even standing position and employ an easy method of locking and unlocking the extending legs. While these essentials may sound so logical, you'll find few tripods that will incorporate all of them. Many excellent European tripods have no device to keep the legs evenly spaced, many American tripods have threaded leglocking collars which are all but immovable even with pliers once they get stuck, and many Japanese tripods are too flimsy. The Tiltall is an excellent tripod in the $50 class. It's sturdy but amazingly light for its beefiness. In addition, it's one of the few tripods which has a head designed for tilting the camera vertically as well as horizontally. Don't buy any tilting head until you put your camera on it and try to take a vertical picture. Most tripods make no provision for vertical shots other than loosening the tripod screw and turning the camera itself. A universal ball and socket joint is preferable to a one-way tilting head.

Electronic flash: I have a great respect for Ascor, Mecablitz, Ultrablitz Braun Hobby, Multiblitz, Hershey and Heiland electronic flash units. They are all well made. If you buy one, make sure you run a test roll of film at various apertures to check the guide numbers. Don't put all your faith in the guide numbers given by the manufacturer. Competition being what it is, manufacturers are apt to attempt slight inflation. A higher-than-proper guide number does not indicate the unit is not good.

My own favorite is the Mighty-Light, a small, compact, rather inexpensive two-piece unit consisting of battery pack and flash head. I like it because it just fits my own purposes. It's equally at home with amateur or professional, it's simple in operation, there hasn't been a need for a new model or radical change in the present one within five years, it has the only universal bounce-flash swivel-head available, and it can be fitted with a ring light. For power you can use high voltage batteries giving 500 flashes in quick succession (my favorites), D-cells, nickel cadmium batteries or AC house current. The best argument I have in its favor however, is five years of use with little or no trouble.

Favorite accessories: 3-ft. long cable release to be used when I want to take pictures of birds close to the nest or birdhouse but wish to stay further away myself.

Accura focusing extension tube which can be used as a focusing mount if you want to use one enlarging lens or other non-focusing lens as a regular camera lens; it's also a fine replacement for a bellows unit.

Polyethylene food storage bags purchaseable in 5 and 10 cent stores make excellent containers for packing lenses, camera bodies without lenses, and other equipment you wish to keep dust-free.

Plastic bowl covers with elastic edges are the best lens caps I've ever used. Any one can fit a whole host of lenses with or without lens hoods. They are removable instantly and fold to nothing.

Lifa filters and filterholders are just about the only units easy to mount and demount from your lens.

Tan paint-masking tape, available in hardware stores, can fasten test sheets and newspaper to walls, fasten film ends to cartridges while bulk loading, be used as labels on anything yet be taken off without leaving a mark. Photographic tape is black and expensive. The Kodak Projection print scale is the simplest method of getting the right exposure for black-and-white enlargements.

I now arrive at the end of this book. Perhaps it would have been well to eliminate pictures or less important information so the traditional peroration could have been added—to go forth, create, interpret, make this a better photographic world. But having long been a photographic editor has hardened my opportunity to it. I can't tell you how to regard your wife, to show your love for your children, or respect your fellow men. This comes only from within. I can only illustrate my own aims as I have tried to use my cameras and techniques to accomplish them.

INDEX